D0955851

BURT FRANKLIN: RESEARCH & SOURCE WORKS SERIES 573
Theatre & Drama Series 12

EARLY
AMERICAN PLAYS

NEW·YORK

FOUNDED IN

MDCCCLXXXV

THE DUNLAP SOCIETY

EARLY
AMERICAN PLAYS
1714-1830

BEING A COMPILATION OF THE TITLES OF PLAYS
BY AMERICAN AUTHORS PUBLISHED AND
PERFORMED IN AMERICA PREVIOUS TO 1830

BY
OSCAR WEGELIN

EDITED WITH AN INTRODUCTION BY
JOHN MALONE

BURT FRANKLIN, NEW YORK

Published by LENOX HILL Pub. & Dist. Co. (Burt **Franklin**)
235 East 44th St., New York, N.Y. 10017
Originally Published: 1900
Reprinted: 1970
Printed in the U.S.A.

S.B.N.: 8337-3721X
Library of Congress Card Catalog No.: 70-130101
Burt Franklin: Research and Source Works Series 573
Theatre and Drama Series 12

Reprinted from the original edition in the New York Public Librar

INTRODUCTION.

D RAMA is neither literature nor amusement. It is
an active social declaration of the yearning for
a place in the eternity of good-knowing and good-
doing. It belongs not to man alone, for it pervades
all life. The evidences of its power with which we
are best informed come of course from the imitative
qualities of man, though it must not be forgotten that
animals and plants make innocent and tragic display
of the same impulses. In the gentle mastery of its
"let's play!" it is the hourly delight of children in the
nursery, and since the Man of Calvary broke the bread
and blessed the wine of His last supper, saying to His
Apostles, *"do this in commemoration of Me!"* it has
been the deeply reverenced and most solemn mystery
of our Christian faith. It lives before and without the
aid of letters. When it calls them to its aid it is not
their servant but their master and their judge. It is
an art so simple that of all arts it is most easily
abused. Its people are despised and degraded and
walk the paths of undeserved obscurity because their
finer impulses are most easily corrupted by pretentious
and false-faced Vanity. Vice in all his walks, from
the throne to the gutter, is prompt to ravin this help-
less art and blast her confiding and unguarded
children.

As one who has given some years to the active study of the drama, its best models and makers, I may take from this little book of titles of early American plays an occasion to review some of the mistakes as well as some of the triumphs which have attended the introduction and patronage of this art among the English-speaking people of America.

During the period of half a century over which the story of this list of American plays extends the government and growth of our country were more busy, more effective, more entirely absorbed in territorial development than in the fostering of social institutions. It was natural, therefore, that dramatic effort by native playmakers should be feeble. The first actors were immigrants and the first plays were those of old country writers. It is most curious to note how stubborn the bent of audiences in this country in favor of the foreign has remained. There are several proverbs about strangers and strange things getting more favor than the home people and their works. When Dunlap began to produce his well-made plays he was forced to adopt the subterfuge of announcing them as works of English authors. Even now an indifferent foreign play can elbow out of the theatre a better work of a native author. I doubt very much whether John Howard Payne would ever have found hearing for his dramatic work had he not gone to England and there gained the approval of the public. No doubt many of the works of these early dramatists were justly relegated to obscurity, but it is quite as surely probable that, had not this strange unliking of home made things so strongly prevailed, the gentle and scholarly men and women who sought to grace the drama of America in the earlier day would have given us many more plays to be proud of.

It will of course be easily understood that as to the drama of English tongue the often used terms "the first play in America" and "the first actors in America" are errors of speech. A century before us the Spaniard had his theatre in Mexico well-supplied with native-born actors of great genius as well as with plays of the mould of Calderon and Lope de Vega made by the scions of three generations of native-born white blood.

When Cortes was allied with the Tlascalans against Montezuma there was in his train a good monk, Fray Toribio de Benevente, who remained in Tlaxcala and acquired the language of the people. In 1538 he produced in that city with native actors several plays on sacred subjects. The third Council of Mexico in 1585 expressly allowed the performance of "sacred histories and other good and soul-helpful matters" under the censorship of the diocesan. The poet Valbuena in 1603 refers to the daily performance of dramas in the City of Mexico as a matter of general knowledge. Thus it seems the Spanish drama of America antedates even the birth of Shakspere.

The French, too, in Louisiana, antedated us in the making of plays. It must then be always kept in mind that the English theatre of America was not a pioneer of the soil. How could it be? When active colonization began the English drama had no legal existence. The statutes of the commonwealth by which the drama of Shakspere was suppressed were still in force. The libertinage which prevailed during the first reign of the Restoration left its stain upon English drama not only in the prevalence of degrading plays but in the corruption of its actors under the example of a profligate king. The healthy tone of Shaksperean drama did not come back to England until the days of Pope and Barton Booth and Macklin.

It is well worth remembering that it was the restoration of Shakspere's text upon the stage, under the studious guidance of such men, that opened a way for the great glory of the stage in the person of Garrick and his school, inherited by the early nineteenth century in America as well as England. In his charming autobiography Captain Alexander Graydon says that the performances of the Hallam Company in Philadelphia, previous to the Revolution, first directed his mind toward the study of Shakspere. Undoubtedly the converse is equally true, and many a good disposition has been turned towards the theatre on account of the reading of this greatest of drama-makers.

It is more to this fact, I believe, than to the merit of early immigrant actors, that the stage of the colonies owes the favor with which it was fostered by the grandsons of Pilgrims and Quakers in spite of inherited prejudice and laws of prohibition established thereon. The question whether it was "Tony" Ashton, Thomas Kean or William and Lewis Hallam who first brought professional players to the colonies

not so important as is the fact that they were cer-
tainly the companions, friends and pupils of David
Garrick who opened the successful course of more
than a century of great plays and players in English-
America with the performance of the Merchant of
Venice in the Theatre at Williamsburg, Virginia, on
the evening of the fifth of September, 1752.

Grave doctors of the Church, wise schoolmen,
lawyers, lawmakers and scholars of this new land
learned quickly to appreciate the truth which a
strange and stupid prejudice too often obscured, that
the proper and only place in which the drama
may be rightly studied is the theatre. The thought
that drama can exist without actors and their coöper-
ative aid is so obvious a contradiction of supposed
conditions that I am astounded when I realize, in lis-
tening to men otherwise sensible, that any one can
fail to see the innate idiocy of such terms as "literary
drama" and "dramatic poem." True it is that the
existence of the thing thus improperly described,
which may be better called "useless and futile literature," serves well to point out by multiplied instances
of failure to reach a point of growth upon the stage,
what true drama ought to be. Think for a moment
how few out of the entire mass of printed dramas in
the English language have lived to take root! No
phrase is more common in the history of the stage than
that of "well-written, but lacks action." So goodbye to
that work as a play. But why make a book of it?
Surely if a wise naval engineer should find upon her
trial that the intricate machine intended for war was

unfit, inadequate and useless for that purpose he would cheerfully and unhesitatingly commend the mass of iron to the moulder's scrap heap, not keep it afloat to confuse the work of well-built battle-ships.

This bibliography of the early American drama affords not many more instances of these mistakes in playmaking than that of any other time or country. Earlier efforts in that direction such as the work of Mr. Godfrey, called the first of our playwrights, but more generally known as son of the inventor of the quadrant, and that of the distinguished jurist, Mr. Tyler, whose honored name is perpetuated as well by the title of an indifferent comedy as by his most valuable opinions from the Bench, would gain little regard had they not been closely followed by the better manuscripts supplied to the stage by Mrs. Susanna Rowson, an actress of the Boston theatre, distinguished as the writer of "Charlotte Temple" (the "Trilby"-book of the last century), John Howard Payne, the precocious and talented boy-actor, whose playing astonished and delighted Great Britain as well as his own country, and whose sweet verse of "Home, Sweet Home!" will not be forgotten while mothers nurse the race of men. The name of William Dunlap naturally follows these in the enumeration of our distinguished playmakers and serves to open the view of a strong purposeful life devoted to the establishment of a lasting home for English drama in these United States.

The honorable career of William Dunlap, the indomitably industrious manager of the New York

Park Theatre, forced at last out of his chosen work by the hard conditions which have attended the theatre as a useful social institution in all its struggles for recognition in this country, is a shameful commentary upon the fatuous carelessness with which American audiences have deserted the drama and its friends in every time of need. Dunlap's disappointment, due only to lack of public support in his darling wish to make a permanent New York play-house where the rules and traditions of good plays would be forever kept and enforced, was exactly parallel to that of Edwin Booth who found himself obliged to give up his noble theatre on Twenty-third street, New York City, in 1874 for the same reason.

The very principle of the theatre demands the generous and ungrudging aid of the public. An audience and their substantial support are indispensable to the play and the play-house. As well expect fire without fuel, or life without food, as good drama without continuous fiscal support. The often uttered cry of modern play purveyors, "Oh! the public want amusement!" is true enough as far as it goes, but it does not justify or palliate that sure degeneracy of the theatre which inevitably attends the apathy of the public in regard to high-class drama. I know well that often the vanity, or jealousy, or selfishness of particular actors has much to do with making a false public sense as to plays, but these conditions as well require a censorship from society as does the representation of vicious and degrading suggestions for the amusement of the profligate and licentious.

Is a censorship of plays then possible to the English stage? Why not? There is now, always has been and will be, a silent and powerful censorship in the healthy and pure-minded disapproval of bad actors and bad playing. Here I mean, too, that the public have and must exercise the right to put off the stage the immoral person and the immoral play. The time, now ripe for a reformation of that censorship, seems to call out for direction toward an effective method of making the power of approval and condemnation vital, vocal, ready and effective for all occasions when good taste or morals are in danger from the misuse of the stage.

From time to time well-meaning people have cried out that the English drama, the theatre of Shakspere, of Garrick, Booth and Siddons should be safeguarded as a social power for good or evil as are the State theatres of France or the royal and imperial companies of the European courts. It is well to note that in the administration of governments where popular suffrage obtains this word "State" is of many meanings, political, geographical, economic and authoritative. In England and the United States there are so many of these differing "states" that it must ever remain impossible to call upon any one of them to establish or maintain such an appanage as a theatre, a simple and easily procured luxury, it is true, but none the less a luxury. A library or an art museum is a luxury. But they and the theatre are useful luxuries and should share equally in the scheme of instructive government. Under the favorite forms of English government (the old country has adopted so many modifications of the rigor of her ancient methods from the successful workings of the Constitutution of the United States that for the purpose of this declaration they may be regarded as coincident and coeffective with ours), there is a political person, with an abundantly provided power, standing next to the people and in full sympathy with them, wherein the right and power to maintain and control the drama may be safely placed. That is the *Municipality*.

The subject of the establishment of municipal theatres has received much attention from the highest sources within the past few years, and principally with regard to our English theatres, from such respectable influences as Sir Henry Irving, the University of Cambridge and the Royal Institute of Great Britain. A short time ago Irving delivered a powerful lecture at Cambridge University on this subject. A lecture was delivered lately by Edwin O. Sachs, an eminent architect and author of the exhaustive work " Modern Theatres and Opera Houses of Europe," before the Royal Institute of Great Britain. The immediate purpose in view at the time of these lectures was the proposition lately taken up by certain public-minded persons in the City of Manchester, England, for the establishment in that place of a municipal theatre upon the plan of endowment and aid adopted in favor of different institutions of the same character upon the Continent of Europe. Mr. Sachs' lecture was delivered before the Society above named on the 12th of February, 1898, and upon the occasion several distinguished persons, members of the Society, discussed the question from all points of view. The general decision was in favor of the municipally-aided establishment. It is an acknowledged plan that the theatre in Manchester will be established, and a trial of continental principles in this regard fully made. This attitude toward the stage, the desire to establish it under State protection by means of a subordinate power, runs in equal step with the history of Christian drama.

To Isabella of Castile the European theatre directly owes its foundation, as a municipal institution. Upon the pacification of her country after the fall of Granada and the expulsion of the Moors in 1492, she submitted to her council and to the learned of the universities the question of the moral value of the drama. Upon receiving from them a favorable judgment, she at once caused to be instituted the "Guild of the Holy Trinity for the Relief of the Sick," with privilege to enroll men and married women for the purpose of giving dramatic performances. Wooden structures called "corrales" were erected by and for the actors, and the principal theatre of the country was long known as "El Corral Real." Our English theatres perpetuate the old Spanish name for the lower floor or yard of the galleried "corral," called by them "el patio," "the yard," and by us the "pit."

From the "Confraternity of the Passion" in France, which established itself in the Hotel de Bourgogne in 1548, came, by the genius of Molière, the be-

ginning of the Comédie Française. This guild was
originally established by Charles VI. in 1402 as an
adjunct of the Hospital of the Trinity, with the
privilege of playing only on Sundays and holidays.

All these guilds, whether in England, France, Spain
or Italy were, at least in their original forms, minis-
terial functions of the State or Municipality, either for
the increase of fiscal charity, the improvement of
methods of religion or celebration of civic anniver-
saries. The idea of an established State Theatre,
though old as the year 342 B. C., when Menander of
Athens put it first into practice, did not take any hold
upon the minds of moderns until the action of Isabella
in Spain. The Elizabethan theatre of Shakspere was
blood-kin to that Spanish institution, and next in point
of origin. Burbage, Laneham, Fletcher and Hey-
wood had their training in the company of players
established by Katharine of Aragon and kept by her
daughter, the Princess Mary. The English theatre
has never been by law recognized as a State institution, but its fosterage by the Court in Shakspere's day
is witnessed, not only by the fact that the Queen
allowed a "cry of players" to call themselves her servants, and contributed to the income of several other
bands, but when, in 1596, the Mayor and Aldermen
of London tried to have the theatre altogether suppressed, the Privy Council declared that the public
exercise of acting by the companies of the Lord Chamberlain, the Lord High Admiral, and of other prominent nobles was necessary in order that the men of
that pleasing quality should be well rehearsed, prac-

ticed and ready to make a good and delectable impression upon the spirits of her sacred Majesty whenever called to the presence for a display of their art.

Permanent theatres were erected in certain European cities as early as 1483, when there was one at Strasbourg which had been erected some time previously by the Syndic or Commune of that city. A similar structure existed at Lyons in 1492, and a curious wood-cut representing the interior, with the curtain down, the minstrel musician piping away from his seat upon the apron of the stage, and the audience assembled, even to the municipal censors in their box, is appended to an edition of the Comedies of Terence, published in that city in the same year. One of the things not the least interesting about this picture is the representation of the Passion of Saint Didymus and the Virgin Dorothea, which forms the lower half of the print. Dorothea, a noble Roman maiden, who was condemned as a Christian to the public brothel, was rescued scatheless by Didymus, a young soldier of the Imperial Guard, who, under pretence of profligacy, visited the cells and persuaded the virgin to escape by aid of his clothes and arms. This pictorial record was probably intended to be a memorial of the popular Action or Mystery often represented with great applause upon the famous stage of the sixteenth century playhouse, in which the devotion and conversion of these young Romans was commemorated. It was at the same time a reminder of the use to which the uncared-for theatre must inevitably fall.

Having in view the perennial growth of the drama, and its unfailing influence upon human nature as a swift and convincing power, teaching by the example of good deeds reproduced to the senses and the judgment by the unique art of the actors, a few States have extended it a much needed helping hand. Much needed, because from the infinite multitude of motives by which human purpose is swayed, those which affect the interests of the theatre may be summed up in three classes: First — Education. Second — Amusement. Third — Luxury. With a commonwealth where the general estimate of the drama gives it the place of an amusement only, the art goes by the most facile descent to the hell of licentiousness and morbid immorality, and, deserted on the stage by all good actors and in the audience by all good men and women, it becomes the mere provoker of lust and procurer of bold and unclean avarice. In states where the fiction of royal dignity and the pomp of privileged classes rule society, the court theatre becomes a mere adjunct of luxury. This tendency ran to its broadest absurdity in the time of the late King of Bavaria, and is the undisguised reason of the existence of the Turkish and Egyptian court theatres. It must be remembered, on the other hand, that in most instances the court theatres of Europe are conducted upon a plan which makes education their actuating motive, yet does not forbid an occasional concession to well-regulated amusement.

Whatever may have been Napoleon's personal motive in framing the Decree of Moscow, by which the State assumed the care of the Théatre Français, he must have looked beyond all prejudice to the dignity of a pure and living art. The history of this famous theatre fully justifies the highest claims made by lovers of the drama for a full correspondence with the best principles of moral education. However foully the French stage may have behaved itself under the guidance of private interests, no blame has ever smirched the House of Molière since it came to be a Government institution. So well known is the story of the Comédie Française, to give this body of actors the traditional name by which they love to call themselves (the legal designation both of the house and of the Institution is "Le Théatre Français"), that it would be perhaps improper for me to give any extended space to it. It relates back as far as the early years of the Seventeenth Century, but had a merely precarious recognition from the Kings of France until the genius of Molière established it under the patronage of the great Cardinal Richelieu in firm and lasting favor. It is now a part of the care of the Minister of Public Instruction and of the Fine Arts, under substantially the same provisions of the Civil Code as those of Napoleon's Decree of Moscow and the law of the year XII (revolutionary period). A committee of the actors of the Théatre Français, who are societaries or sharers, regulates the affairs of the Institution under the presidency of a General Director appointed by the Minister of Public Instruction and Fine Arts.

It is a very significant fact, and may be connected

with the proposition that when a people begin to degenerate the first symptom of their decline is found in the muddiness of their drama; that the Latin races, particularly the Spanish and Italian, have for the last quarter of a century generally regarded the theatre and its work as a place and an occasion of social rendezvous, rather than as an opportunity of study and improvement, while in Austria, Germany, Russia, Denmark, Sweden and Norway, the drama has been placed under the protection of the crown or the local government, and thus safeguarded against the intrusion of speculators, skilled only in the barter of soiled clothing, with meretricious dispositions to make money by catering to the taste of the vicious and debased. The survival of a prejudice derived from Puritanical influences, first asserted in England upon the establishment of the Commonwealth, when all institutions and traditions of the drama in English speech were swept away by the strict legislation of Cromwell and his party, has retarded, both in England and America, all efforts toward the restoration of the English drama to that position of dignity and self-respect which is its inheritance from Nature, and should be the reward of the devotion of its champions.

In this regard it is well to observe that the most successful theatres are to be found among the people of the Teutonic race. When the present Emperor of Germany had reached the tenth anniversary of his accession to the kingly and imperial dignity, among other notable actions, he took occasion to express his good-will toward the royal players. When complimented upon the occasion by the members of the Berlin Royal Theatre, the Emperor said to them:

"The theatre should be the instrument of the monarch, and like the school and the university, work for the presentation of the highest spirit and qualities of our noble Fatherland."

In this expression of good-will, whatever may have been the ulterior purpose behind it, there rests a very dignified tradition of history.

Germany began to have regular players about 1626, when some students of the Universities of Jena and Leipsic founded a company under the direction of John Welten, who, before turning player, was a Professor of Philosophy, as was his father, in the University of Jena in Saxony. Welten's company was taken into the service of the Elector of Saxony and became the model of German playing companies until the establishment of the Prussian Theatre, under the management of the poet Iffland, about one hundred years later. The master-singers of Nuremburg, Mayence, Strasburg, Augsburg and notably the influence of the shoemaker poet, Hans Sachs, during the same period assisted materially in the ultimate elevation of German drama to court and municipal protection. The only theatre in the United States which has preserved the dignity and the traditions of a well organized stock company of skilled and able actors is a modest little German house in New York City where a few people of taste in the metropolis have come to learn with shame for their time and language that the best performances on the American stage are given to-day in German.

Sometimes it happens that an amiable and public-spirited mind holds out to the drama, either by bequest or gift, the aid of substantial and unselfish financial endowment. Unfortunately such instances are rare. Two or three in which racial causes actuated the endowment and support of theatres exist in the German and Czech Theatres in Prague and the Slav Theatre in Laibach. These are in different provinces of Austria. The German Theatre at Prague, which seats 1,800 persons, was built by the subscription of private persons who were desirous of asserting the influence of the German language against the national speech of Bohemia. When in 1887 the old National Theatre, in which a Bohemian company had been domiciled, was destroyed by fire, an association formed for the purpose of fostering the Czech language and traditions appealed for a popular subscription to rebuild the theatre, £94,000 was raised in six weeks, and in two years a fine modern structure seating 2,000 persons and costing £253,000, was opened. In 1892 the Slavic population of Laibach, fired by the example of the people of Prague, built, at a cost of £20,000, by popular subscription a fine theatre capable of seating 1,000 persons, on the site of an older one burned in 1887. The action of the people of Laibach is more significant from the fact that the population of the town is only 30,000.

The Teatro Internazionale Lirico at Milan, built in 1894 in place of the old Teatro Canobiana, owes its existence to the munificence of a public-spirited man of wealth, Signor Edoardo Lonzogo, who bears the expense of maintaining it.

It is not perhaps generally known that the U. S. Federal Government sustains a certain number of theatres which have been built and are almost entirely supported with public moneys. There are three of these, and they are part of the National Soldiers' Homes. There is one at Taugus, Maine; another at Hampton, Virginia, and a third at Dayton, Ohio. These theatres are under the management of the Commandants of the respective posts, and are occupied from time to time by companies of actors engaged by the Commandant, either for a single performance or for a series. Admission to such performances is always given to the public upon the payment of the usual price for seats which obtains in the locality, but the inmates of the institution are admitted either freely, or upon the payment of a nominal fee of five or ten cents.

Until the days of general confusion, "the late innovation" under Henry VIII., the governing idea of public drama in England was paternal responsibility of the municipal fathers therefor. The plays of Coventry, Chester and York were not, as is commonly supposed, performed by the monks of their vicinage, but by the men and boys belonging or apprenticed to trade guilds playing under the fiscal direction of the town officers, aided by the religious only as to matters of speech and music. In the new order which came about from the succession of Elizabeth, the drama went under private patronage, not because such a condition was thought better, but because the

social power of the parish was broken by the aggran-
dizement to the crown of church fiefs and fortunes;
and as the people are fondly attached to their drama
the State assumed by indirection its care and control.

James I. was, at least in the early and much prom-
ising days of his reign, a bit bolder in resisting the
Puritanic prejudice against the drama. He gave
Shakspere and his fellows a royal patent as servants
of the household and the players were King's officers
until the end of the reign of Charles I. and his war
with the Parliament. The English drama has not
yet recovered from the shock it suffered from the
headsman's axe at Whitehall on the 30th of January,
1649.

It is a fact that the English-speaking race, inheri-
ting the common law, literature, traditions, religion
and institutions of the mother land, though united
always with an everywhere indulgent good humor, has
been, by one or other of these influences, kept in the
channel of that mistaken dislike for the theatre so
often expressed by ill-instructed or fanatical preachers
of the hard-hitting Ironsides. A superficial reading
of Tertullian in the school of a new direction of
religious thought impressed the minds of many with
the conviction that all exercise of the art of drama
was pomp of Satan; ignoring the fact, always to be
kept in mind in the study of the attitude of the
Fathers of the Church toward the theatre, that in
their day the places of public shows were devoted to the
worship of heathen deities, and that the performance
and its attendance were acts of adherence to Pagan
religion. It has been pointed out time after time in

the councils of Church and State that this view must
not be held with regard to the exercise of the drama
in Christian countries. No safer guide upon this
proposition can be cited than the words of St. Thomas
of Aquin in dealing with this subject. He, in terms,
declared that the drama is an elevating and inspiring
art, greatly conducive to human improvement and
good will, and is therefore to be cultivated and protected.

The methods of both the Federal and State
Governments in the United States properly exclude
the thought of either National or State theatres. No
such exclusion can exist with regard to a municipal
corporation. The State, it is true, must be asked to
place upon its statute books an empowering provision
before any municipality can apply moneys for such a
purpose. The only difficulty in the way of such
action is one of politics, which, let us hope, may in
time be removed by rooting up mistaken prejudices
against the theatre as an institution.

The objection that such action would be an unwar-
ranted interference with private business has long
since been invalidated. The bookseller might as
well urge the same reason against the public library,
or the circus against the maintenance of menageries.
The successful and useful municipally aided theatres
of continental Europe have not only made the drama
better and more respected in their communities, but
have improved the business of private theatres by
ridding them of meretricious competition. During
the ten years of his control of New York's best

theatre William Dunlap wrote and produced nearly
sixty plays.   They were not all, perhaps, excellent
or entirely original, but they were fruits of an unselfish devotion to the upbuilding of drama in his
native country.   He gave up his heroic struggle for
the independence of the American theatre in 1805.
Had any of the spirit which recognizes the drama as
a social and enlightening power taken hold of the
makers of old New York, this Society and its work
would now be homed in a municipally protected
theatre of his foundation.

The following list of plays grew out of the patient
and praiseworthy work of Mr. Oscar Wegelin among
various and widely dispersed sources of information as
to dramas printed before 1830.   In making his valuable list that gentleman spent two years in correspondence with important libraries and in carefully
comparing book-lists.   With the approval of Mr.
Douglas Taylor, the Society's honored and distinguished President, I have added to Mr. Wegelin's list
the titles, with dates and places of performance of plays
acted but not published, together with brief memoirs
of their authors where known, in order that the book
may be as complete a record of early American plays
and dramatic authorship as, from all sources of information, it seems possible to make.   The effect intended
is to frame a history of the friends of American drama
in its early struggles.   Beginning when the mighty
causes were at work which brought a free people
through two hard-fought and successful wars, it is not
to be wondered at that much of this early drama is

useless to posterity, made up as it is of skits and satires upon the politics and social differences of the time. Except some of the plays of Dunlap adapted from safe and approved foreign originals, similar works of John Howard Payne, James Nelson Barker's dramatization of *Marmion*, George Washington Parke Custis' *Pocahontas* and Stone's *Metamora*, there is little in the whole list which would bear reproduction, or be of use more than to suggest motives for new scenes. Of the plays which remained in manuscript, beyond the record of their production with here and there a short note of the story and the work of the players, there are only fragmentary remains. It may be set down as a safe rule of judgment as to dramatic quality that the plays which were printed were fit for no more than the use to which an indulgent Providence and the Dunlap Society have dedicated them—to serve as examples of the good-will and sympathy with which a few great and good men in the days of our country's fiery trial held out their helping hands to the gentle art of drama.

NEW YORK,   JOHN MALONE.
       April, 1900.

Early American Plays.

ANONYMOUS PLAYS.

Alfred the Great.   An Historical Tragedy, in Five
Acts, by a Young Gentleman of this City.
>   16mo, pp 107.   *New York*, 1822.

Americana; or, A New Tale of the Genii. Being an Allegorical Mask in Five Acts.
>   8vo, pp 128. *Baltimore*, 1822.   Dedicated to Thomas Jef-
ferson.

The Battle of Brooklyn.   A Farce in Two Acts,
as it was performed on Long Island on Tuesday,
the 27th day of August, 1776, by the Representa-
tives of the Tyrants of America assembled at Philadelphia.   (6 lines of poetry.)
>   *New York*, printed for J. RIVINGTON, in the Year of the
Rebellion, 1776.
>   Reprinted in Brooklyn.   8vo, 1873.

The Battle of Eutaw Springs.   A Drama in Five
Acts.
>   8vo, pp 52.   *Charleston* (circa 1790).
>   A play with a similar title was written by W. IOOR.

The Better Sort; or, The Girl of Spirit. A Farce.
>   8vo, pp iv.–80. *Boston*, 1789.

The Blockheads; or, The Affrighted Officers.
A Farce.

    12mo, pp 19 (2).   *Boston*, Queen Street, 1776.
    Also, 16mo, pp v.–43.   *New York*, 1782.
    Attributed to Mrs. MERCY WARREN.

The Blockheads; or, Fortunate Contractor.
An Opera in Two Acts. As it was performed at
New York [during the Revolution].

    8vo, pp v.–43.   *New York*, printed; *London*, reprinted
for G. KEARSLEY. 1782. 2 Plates.

Blow for Blow. A Tragedy.

    Baltimore, 1805.

Catharine Brown, the Converted Cherokee.
A Missionary Drama, founded on fact. By a Lady.

    12mo, pp 27.   *New Haven*, 1819.

Columbia and Britannia. A Dramatic Piece, by
a Citizen of the United States.

    8vo, pp 63.   *New London:* Printed by T. GREEN, 1786.
    Among the Characters in this play are Fabius (Washington) and Perjuris (Arnold).

Dramatic Pieces Calculated to exemplify the
mode of conduct which will render young ladies
both amiable and happy, when their school education is completed. In three Volumes.

    12mo. *New Haven:* Printed by ABEL MORSE. 1791.
    The prefaces to these works are signed P. I.
    Contents. Vol. 1. The Good Mother-in-Law, the Good
Daughter-in-Law.
    Vol. 2. The Reformation, The Maternal Sister: a Drama
in three acts.
    Vol. 3. The Triumph of Reason, The Contrast. Each
piece is paged separately.

An Exercise, Containing a Dialogue and Two Odes. Performed at the Public Commencement in the College of Philadelphia, November 17, 1767.

> 4to, pp 8. *Philadelphia:* Printed by WILLIAM GODDARD, 1767.

An Exercise; Containing a Dialogue and Two Odes. Set to music, for the Public Commencement, in the College of Philadelphia, May 17th, 1775.

> 8vo, pp 8. *Philadelphia:* Printed by JOSEPH CRUIKSHANK, 1775.

Federalism Triumphant in the Steady Habits of Connecticut Alone; or, The Turnpike Road to a Fortune. A Comic Opera, or Political Farce in Six Acts, as performed at the Theatres Royal and Aristocratic at Hartford and New Haven, October, 1801.

> 8vo, pp 40. n. p. Printed in the year 1802.

The Female Enthusiast. A Tragedy in Five Acts, by a Lady.

> 12mo, pp 51. *Charleston,* J. HOFF, 1807.

The French Revolution; including a Story, Founded in Fact, of Leontine and Matilda. A Drama. Written and Exhibited in the United Fraternity, at Dartmouth, 1790; Exhibited also at Windsor, Vermont, May, 1791.

> 8vo, pp 67. Printed at New Bedford, Massachusetts, by JOHN SPOONER, 1793.

The Indian Prophecy.

> 12mo. *Georgetown, D. C.,* 1823.

Indoctum Parliamentum. A Farce, in One Act, and a beautiful variety of scenes.

> 12mo, pp 7. n. p. (1818).
> Refers to a law enacted by the Legislature of New York, on the petition of Eunice Chapman, a Shaker, to have the marriage contract between herself and husband dissolved. Among the characters introduced are: " General Radix " (Erastus Root), " His dis-orderly Sergeant " (Dr. Sergeant), "Lignum" (Speaker Wood), etc.

The Intolerants. Three First Acts of Things Among Us; as performed at the . . . . . . with more effect than applause.

> 12mo, pp 26. *Philadelphia*, 1827.

The Italian Husband. A Dramatic Poem.

> This piece is part of a book entitled " Lays of Leisure, The Italian Husband, The Young Dreamer, a Fugitive Offering in Verse."
> *Philadelphia:* JESPER HARDING, 1825.

Jefferson and Liberty. A Celebration of the 4th of March; a Patriotic Tragedy; a Picture of Corrupt Administration, in Five Acts, written by Nichols.

> 12mo, pp 29. n. p. Sold at the Printing Office, Temple Street, 1801.
> " Nichols " is probably a pseudonym.

Jonathan in England. A Comedy.

> 12mo, pp 32. *Boston* (circa 1828).
> This play is a version of Colman's " Who Wants a Guinea ? " and was performed at the Park Theatre, New York, December 3, 1828.

The Military Glory of Great Britain. An Entertainment given by the late candidates for Bache-

lor's Degree at the close of the Anniversary Commencement held in Nassau Hall, New Jersey,
September 27th, 1762.

8vo, pp 15. *Philadelphia:* Printed by WILLIAM BRAD-
FORD, 1762.

The Monthly Assembly. A Farce.
8vo, *Boston*, 1770.

The Motley Assembly. A Farce. Published for
the Entertainment of the Curious.
12mo, pp 15. *Boston*, N. COVERLY, 1799.
Attributed to Mrs. MERCY WARREN.

**Nature and Philosophy; or, The Youth Who
Never Saw a Woman.** A Drama adapted from
the French, by a Citizen of Richmond.
12mo. *Richmond*, 1821.
Played at the Park Theatre, New York, December 10, 1821.

The Night Watch; or, The Pirate's Den. A
Melodrama by a Gentleman of Boston.
18mo, pp 34. *Boston*, 1820.

**Occurrences of the Times; or, The Transac-
tions of Four Days.** A Farce.
16mo, pp 23. *Boston*, 1789.

The Patriots. A Comedy in Five Acts.
Philadelphia, [n. d.]
Published during the Revolution.

The Paxton Boys. A Farce. Translated from
the original French, by a Native of Donegall.
Folding Plate. The second edition.
Sm. 8vo, pp. 16. *Philadelphia:* Printed and Sold by
ANTHONY ARMBRUSTER, 1764.

Philip; or, The Aborigines. A Drama.
  12mo, pp 48. *New York*, 1822.

The Plan of a Performance of Solemn Music. To be in the Hall of the College of Philadelphia, on Wednesday Evening, April 10th, 1765. For the Benefit of the Charity Schools.
  8vo, pp 4. [n. p. n. d.]

The Politicians; or, A State of Things. A Dramatic Piece. Written by an American, and a Citizen of Philadelphia.
  8vo, pp 37. *Philadelphia:* Printed for the author, 1798.

Sans Souci, Alias Free and Easy; or, An Evening's Peep into a Polite Circle. An Intire New Entertainment, in Three Acts.
  8vo, pp 24. *Boston:* Printed by WARDEN and RUSSELL, 1785.
  Second Edition. 8vo, Boston, 1785.

Saul. A Dramatic Sketch.
  This piece is probably by N. P. WILLIS. It was published in the *American Monthly Magazine* for June, 1829.

A Scene In the First Act of the New Farce. Published as a Specimen. [Philadelphia] Printed: In the first Year of the new Hegira Secundus, the Paxtonian Expedition.
  Sm. 8vo, pp 8. (*Philadelphia*): Printed by ANTHONY ARMBRUSTER, (1764).

Shepherdess of the Alps. A play in Four Acts, by a Citizen of New York.
  12mo, pp 51. *New York*, 1815.

The Sultana; or, A Trip to Turkey. A Melodrama in Three Acts, founded on Lord Byron's Don Juan.
> 12mo, pp 34. *New York,* 1822.

The Suspected Daughter; or, Jealous Father. A Farce in Three Acts, both Serious and Comic, written by T. T.
> *Boston,* 1751.
> This is probably the first play written by a native American.

Sylla. A Tragedy, in Five Acts, as represented at the Theatre Français, at Paris, by E. Jouy, member of the Institute. Translated from the French, by a Citizen of New York.
> 16mo, pp 69. *New York,* 1826.
> Performed at the Chatham Theatre, 1827.

Theodora. A Dramatic Sketch, in Two Acts.
> [n. p. n. d.]

Tricks of the Times; or, The World of Quacks. A Farce of domestic origin.
> 12mo, *New York,* 1819.
> A satire on New Yorkers of the day.

Two Pages of Frederick the Great. A Farce in Three Acts.
> 16mo. *New York,* 1826.

Xerxes the Great.
> 12mo. Printed by T. H. PALMER, *Philadelphia,* 1815.

102; or, The Veteran and His Progeny.
> 16mo, pp 33. *Boston,* 1828.

IN MANUSCRIPT.

American Captive, The. Altered from " The Sultan." A Farce.

    Played at the John Street Theatre, New York, February 29, 1796.

American Tars. (The Purse.)

    Played in the Park Theatre, New York, January 29, 1798.

Ancient Soldier, The.

Battle of North Point, The.

    Played in Baltimore, Md.

Capture of Major André.

    Played in Baltimore.

Down East; or, The Militia Training. A Farce.

    Played at the Park Theatre, April 17, 1830.

Festival of Peace, The. A Patriotic Allegory.

    Played at the Park Theatre, New York, February 20, 1815. This was in honor of the Treaty of Peace between Great Britain and the United States.

Greece and Liberty.

The Green Mountain Boys.

    Played at the New Park Theatre, New York, February 22, 1822.

Guilt. Translated from the German.

Harlequin Panatahah; or, The Genii of the Algonquins.

    Played at the Park Theatre, New York, January 4, 1809.

Harper's Daughter, The. A translation of Schiller's " Cabal and Love."

The Indian Wife.
>Played at the Park Theatre, New York, June 4, 1830.

The Irish Patriot.

The Jubilee; or, Triumph of Freedom.

The Lad of Spirit; or, The Fool of Fortune.
>Played at the Park Theatre, New York, April, 1798.

The Last of the Serpent Tribe.
>Played in New Orleans, La.

Life in New York; or, Firemen on Duty.

Love in a Cloud.

Lucinda.

The Manhattoes.   An Indian Drama.
>Played at the Park Theatre, New York, June 13, 1829.

The Medium; or, Happy Tea Party.
>Played in Boston in 1796.

Miantonomah and Narrahmattah.   From Cooper's "Wept of Wish-ton-Wish."
>*New York* and *London.*
>Played at the Park Theatre, January 15, 1830.

The Pilot.

Pioneers, The.   From Cooper's novel of the same name.
>Played at the New Park Theatre, New York, April 21, 1833.

The Poor Student.

Return from the Camp, The.

2

Ruffian Boy. Dramatized from Burroughs' "Shakespeare in Love."
   Played in Boston.

A Tale of the Crusade. Tragedy played in New York.

Thirty-Three John Street. A Farce.
   Played at the Park Theatre, New York, January 21, 1830.

The Wigwam; or, Templeton Manor. From Cooper's "Pioneers."
   Played at the Park Theatre, New York, July 5, 1830.

BARKER, JAMES NELSON.

JAMES NELSON BARKER, born in Philadelphia in 1784, died 1858, was originally in the army as a captain of artillery, and served in the war of 1812. He was afterwards an Alderman and then Mayor of the city of Philadelphia. He wrote a work called "Sketches of the Primitive Settlements on the River Delaware," and was a contributor to the *Atlantic Souvenir.—J. M.*

The Indian Princess. An Operatic Melodrama. Founded on an Incident in Smith's "Virginia."
   18mo, pp iv.-74. *Philadelphia*, 1808.
   First acted in Philadelphia, April 6, 1808. Reproduced at the Park Theatre, New York, June 14, 1809.
   This is the story of Pocahontas and Captain John Smith.

Tears and Smiles. A Comedy in Five Acts, performed at the Theatre, Philadelphia, March 4, 1807.
   18mo, pp 85. *Philadelphia*, 1808.

Marmion; or, The Battle of Flodden Field. A Drama.

18mo, pp vii.–79. *New York*, 1816.

Played at the Park Theatre, New York, April 13, 1812.

An adaptation of Scott's " Marmion." When it was played at the Park Theatre, New York, from the prejudice then existing against American plays, it was announced as the production of an English author, Thomas Morton, "received with unbounded applause in London." It was enthusiastically received, and had a long lease of popularity.

How to Try a Lover. A Comedy.

16mo, pp 67. *New York*, 1817.

Superstition. A Tragedy.

12mo, pp 68. *Philadelphia*, [n. d.] (1823).

Played in Philadelphia, Pa., 1824.

The Travellers.

Philadelphia, 1809.

IN MANUSCRIPT.

America. A Mask in One Act.

Attila. A Tragedy (written in 1805, and left unfinished).

Armourer's Escape, The; or, Three Years at Nootka Sound. A Melodramatic Sketch in Two Acts.

Played in Philadelphia, March 24, 1817.

Founded on the adventures of an American sailor who was engaged by the management to play the principal part in the drama. His three years in the Nootka country did not ensure for him a career upon the stage.—*J. M.*

The Embargo; or, What News?
Played in Philadelphia, March 16, 1808.

BARTON, ANDREW.

See Colonel Thomas Forrest.

The Disappointment; or, The Force of Credulity. A new American Comic Opera of Two Acts.
12mo, pp 56. *New York*, 1767.
Another Edition, 16mo, pp iv.-95. *Philadelphia*, 1796.
"Air No. IV. is Yankee Doodle."— SABIN.

BEACH, L.

Jonathan Postfree; or, The Honest Yankee. A Musical Farce in Three Acts.
12mo, *New York*, 1807.

BELL, D. V.

IN MANUSCRIPT.

The Fair Maid of Perth.
Played at the Lafayette Theatre, New York (date unknown), and at the New Bowery, June 17, 1829.

BIDWELL, BARNABAS.

BARNABAS BIDWELL, born in Tyringham (now Monterey), Mass., August 23, 1763; died in Kingston,

Canada, July 27, 1833, was the second son of Rev. Adonijah Bidwell. Graduated from Yale in 1785, and was made LL.D. by Brown University in 1805. He settled in Stockbridge, Mass., in 1793, and was successively Treasurer of Berkshire County, Attorney-General of the State, and Member of Congress. His residence in Canada resulted from his responsibility for some irregularity in his business as a banker.

The Mercenary Match. A Tragedy.

12mo, pp 57. *New Haven*, MEIGS, BOWEN, & DANA. (1785.)

This piece was performed by students of Yale College.

BISBEE, NOAH, Jr.

The History of the Falcos. A Comedy in Four Acts; Part First.

12mo, pp 137. *Walpole, N. H.:* Printed for the Author at the Observatory Press, 1808.

BOTSFORD, MRS.

The Reign of Reform; or, Yankee Doodle Court. By a Lady.

18mo, pp 146. *Baltimore:* Printed for the Authoress, 1830.

A Dialogue. The Characters personating distinguished individuals of the day.

A Continuation of the above. 18mo, pp 79. (1.) *Baltimore*, 1830.

BRAY, JOHN.

The Tooth Ache; or, Mistakes of a Morning.
12mo. *Philadelphia*, 1814.

BRECK, CHARLES.

CHARLES BRECK, born in Boston, Mass., 1782; died at Amsterdam, Holland, May, 1822, was the third son of Samuel Breck, a wealthy merchant of Boston, who was agent to the army and fleet of King Louis XVI. after the French intervention in the American Revolution. Charles Breck, while travelling in Italy, met and became engaged to a very beautiful young lady of that country. He built in Philadelphia, whither his father had removed from Boston, a residence exactly like that of his betrothed. Her sudden death, just before his arrival in Europe to claim his bride, hastened his own.— *J. M.*

The Fox Chase. A Comedy in Five Acts, as performed at the Theatres, Philadelphia and Baltimore.
18mo, pp 64. *New York*, 1808.

The Trust. A Comedy in Five Acts.
18mo, pp 82. *New York*, 1808.

BRECKENRIDGE, HUGH HENRY.

HUGH HENRY BRECKENRIDGE, born near Campbelton, Scotland, in 1748; died in Carlyle, Pa., June 25, 1816. He came with his parents to America when

only five years of age, was graduated from Princeton in 1771, and continued as a tutor in that college.
He next studied divinity, and took charge of an
academy in Maryland; was editor of "The United
States Magazine" in Philadelphia in 1776, and a chap-
lain in the American army in the war of the Revolution. He afterwards studied law under Samuel Chase.
In 1781 he crossed the Alleghanies, established himself at Pittsburg, took an active part in the Whiskey
Insurrection, and after that affair was over took pains
to vindicate his conduct by the publication of "Inci-
dents of the Insurrection in the Western Parts of
Pennsylvania." He was afterwards Judge of the Su-
preme Court of Pennsylvania.

The Battle of Bunker Hill. A Dramatic Piece
of Five Acts, in heroic measure; by a Gentleman
of Maryland.

> Pulchrumque mori succurrit in armis,
> 'Tis glorious to die in battle.— *Virgil.*

Philadelphia: Printed and sold by ROBERT BELL, in Third
Street, 1776.

This play was recited by Breckenridge's pupils in 1776.
It was dedicated to Robt. Stockton. The principal charac-
ters are well-known officers in the American and British
Armies.

**The Death of General Montgomery, at the
Siege of Quebec.** A Tragedy, with an Ode in
honor of the Pennsylvania Militia, and the small
band of regular Continental troops who sustained

the campaign in the depth of winter, January, 1777, and repulsed the British forces from the banks of the Delaware. To which are added Elegiacal Pieces, commemorative of Distinguished Characters.

8vo, pp 79. (5.) Frontispiece. *Philadelphia:* Printed and sold by ROBERT BELL, 1777.

Another Edition. 8vo, pp 68. *Norwich*, J. TRUMBULL. 1777.

BROWN, CHARLES BROCKDEN.

CHARLES BROCKDEN BROWN, born in Philadelphia, Pa., January 17, 1771; died there, February 22, 1810, was originally intended for the bar, but gave up that study for literature about 1796. He soon took rank as a novelist of the first class, and was the first American to take that place in English literature. His first writings were published in Philadelphia periodicals, notably "The Rhapsodist," which appeared in "The Columbian Magazine." He published "The Monthly Magazine" and "American Review" (1779–1799), and edited "The Literary Magazine" and "American Register" from 1803 to 1808. He was with Dunlap and Dr. Elihu Hubbard Smith, a member of the "Friendly Club" in New York, and one of Dunlap's most devoted friends. He was one of the first to advocate (in 1803) the purchase of Louisiana from France; and in a series of articles published in that year strongly urged the progressive territorial extension of the Union. He was married in November,

1804, to Miss Elizabeth Linn, daughter of Rev. Dr. William Linn of New York, and thus became the brother-in-law of John Blair Linn, between whom and himself a lifelong attachment of affection existed.

J. M.

Alcuin.   A Dialogue on the Rights of Women.
16mo.   *New York*, 1797.

BROWN, DAVID PAUL.

DAVID PAUL BROWN, born in Philadelphia in 1795; died in 1875, studied law and was admitted to the bar in 1816.   He contributed in early life to a number of magazines, and wrote "The Prophet of St. Paul's," Philadelphia, 1836; "The Trial," a tragedy, and a farce called "Love and Honor."   The two last were not acted, and probably not published.   He was also the author of legal works.   Besides the play mentioned below, he wrote and published a number after 1830, not included in this list.

Sertorius; or, The Roman Patriot.   A Tragedy.
8vo, pp 87.   *Philadelphia*, 1830.

BURGOYNE, GENERAL JOHN.

JOHN BURGOYNE, born about 1730; died in London, England, June 4, 1792, was a natural son of Lord Bingley.   Having entered the army at an early age, he made a runaway match with a daughter of the Earl of Derby, and by the favor of that alliance was greatly advanced in his profession. He was a brigadier-general in Portugal in 1762, and a member of Parliament from Midhurst Borough from 1761. His alleged political discrepancies were roughly handled by Junius. He was appointed to a command in America when the War of Independence began in 1775, and was in Boston during the battle of Bunker Hill. In 1777 he led an army from Canada into New York, but was compelled to surrender his forces to the Continental Generals Gates and Arnold at Saratoga. He went to England on parole in May, 1778, and took a position against the ministry in Parliament. An effort was made to exclude him as a prisoner of war, but failed, whereupon he resigned his military rank. After the treaty of peace with the Americans, he was restored to his rank in the army, and made Commander-in-chief in Ireland. After two years there he gave up public life, and became devoted to literature. He wrote a vaudeville, "The Maid of the Oaks," in 1774; produced a comic opera, "The Lord of the Manor," in 1780, and in 1786 wrote a comedy called "The Heiress." In addition to these he was the author of many works in poetry and prose.—*J. M.*

IN MANUSCRIPT.

The Blockade of Boston.

Played in Boston in 1776.

During the performance of this play by the British soldiers in Boston, before the evacuation, at a date which is not given, but probably in March, 1776, in one of the scenes a sergeant came suddenly on the stage in great excitement, and shouted: "The rebels! the rebels! They are attacking the Neck!" The audience wildly applauded what they took to be a fine bit of acting. The drums soon beat to arms and stopped the play.

BURK, JOHN DALY.

JOHN DALY BURK, born in Ireland about 1776; died in 1808, became, while at Trinity College, Dublin, an ardent politician, and involved himself in difficulties with the authorities. It is said he belonged to a secret political society which tried to rescue a rebel on his way to execution. Burk took shelter in a bookseller's shop, while his wolf-dog kept the police at bay. Escaping in woman's apparel, given him by a Miss Daly, whose name he afterwards added to his own, he came to America, settled in Boston, and became editor of a newspaper called "The Polar Star and Boston Daily Advertiser." He afterwards settled in New York, and published a paper called "The Time-Piece." Arrested on a charge of publishing a libel contrary to the provisions of the Sedition Law of 1798, he left New York and settled at Petersburg, Va. In 1804 he published a "History of Virginia," in 4 vols., the fourth being issued after his death. He also wrote a "History of the Late War in Ireland, with an Account of the United Irish Association, from the First Meeting in Belfast, to the Landing of the French at Killala," published in Philadelphia, 1799. Also, "An Historical Essay on the Character and Antiquity of Irish Songs," published in "The Richmond Enquirer," May, 1808. He was killed in a duel with a Frenchman named Coquebert.

Bunker Hill; or, The Death of General Warren. An Historic Tragedy, in Five Acts. by John Burk, Late of Trinity College, Dublin, as played at the Theatres in America, for fourteen nights, with unbounded applause.

Copyright secured according to law.

12mo, pp 55. *New York:* Printed by T. GREENLEAF, MDCCXCVII.

Another Edition. 16mo, pp 39. *Baltimore,* 1808.

Same: 12mo, pp 44. *New York,* 1817.

Reprinted by the Dunlap Society.

This play was first played at the Haymarket in Boston, February 17, 1798. It was also played a number of times in New York.

The Death of General Montgomery. A Tragedy.

12mo, pp 68. *Philadelphia,* 1797.

Female Patriotism; or, The Death of Joan d'Arc. An Historic Play in Five Acts.

12mo, pp 40. *New York,* 1798.

Played at the New Park Theatre, New York, 1798.

Bethlem Gabor, Lord of Transylvania; or, The Man-Hating Palatine. An Historical Drama, in Three Acts.

16mo, pp 49. *Petersburg,* 1807.

IN MANUSCRIPT.

Joan of Arc; or, The Maid of Orleans. A Tragedy.

Played at the Park Theatre, New York, April 13, 1798.

Fortunes of Nigel. A Dramatization of Scott's Novel.

> Played at the Park Theatre, New York, June 30, 1823.

Innkeeper of Abbeville.

Which Do You Like Best?

CARR, MRS.

IN MANUSCRIPT.

The Fair American.

> Played at the John Street Theatre, New York, November 9, 1789.

CHAPMAN, SAMUEL HENRY.

SAMUEL HENRY CHAPMAN, born in London, May 10, 1799; died in Philadelphia, May 16, 1830, was an actor as well as dramatist. He made his first appearance on the stage at Covent Garden Theatre, London, as *Agib* in "Timour, the Tartar." He was brought to the United States in 1827 by Mr. Francis Courtney Wemyss, manager of the Chestnut Street Theatre, Philadelphia, in company with Mr. and Mrs. Sloman, Mrs. Austin, and Miss Emery, for the stock company of that theatre. His début was made October 31, 1837, as *Pierre* in "Venice Preserved." He became a favorite immediately, and of him it is said he had no equal in heroic rôles in his time. In May, 1829, he became joint manager of the Walnut Street Theatre. He married Elizabeth Jefferson, daughter of the elder and aunt of the now living Joseph Jefferson, in the

same year.   While riding, to illustrate to an artist the
scene of the robbery in Turner's Lane in his own play
of " The Mail Coach," he was thrown from his horse,
and so injured that he died within a week.   It is said
his hurt was aggravated greatly by the fact that he
continued to play every night, and having a piece of
brass armor next his skin, blood-poisoning was caused
in his wounded shoulder.— *J. M.*

The Red Rover.   A Drama founded on J. F.
   Cooper's novel of that name.
      18mo, pp 52.   *Philadelphia*, N. D.
      Played at Chestnut Street Theatre, Philadelphia, 1828.

IN MANUSCRIPT.

Doctor Foster.

Gasparoni.

The Mail Coach.

CLINCH, CHARLES POWELL.

CHARLES POWELL CLINCH, born in New York City
in 1797 ; died there December 16, 1880, was a
son of a wealthy ship-chandler, and in his early life
was private secretary to Henry Eckford, the well-
known ship-builder, at whose house he met many of
the best literary men of the time.   He became very
prominent and successful as an editorial writer and
dramatic critic.   The loss of his fortune from invest-
ments in insurance company stocks depreciated by

the great fire in New York City in 1835, caused him to accept an appointment in the New York Custom-House, where he remained for forty years as Deputy, and finally Assistant Collector of the port. He resigned in 1876.— *J. M.*

IN MANUSCRIPT.

The Spy. A Dramatization of James Fenimore Cooper's novel of the same name.
> Played at the Park Theatre, New York, March 1, 1822.

The Expelled Collegian. A Farce.
> Played at the Park Theatre, New York, May 24, 1822.

The Avenger's Vow.
> Played at the Park Theatre, New York, February 25, 1823.

First of May in New York; or, Double or Quit. A Farce.
> Played at the Park Theatre, New York, February 25, 1830.

COCKINGS, GEORGE.

GEORGE COCKINGS, born in Devonshire, England; died February 6, 1802, lived a great part of his time in Dartmouth, England, and from there went first to Newfoundland, where he passed several years, then to Boston, where he held some small position under the English Government. For thirty years in England he held the place of Register of the Society of Arts, Manufacturing and Commerce in the Adelphi. He wrote "War, An Heroic Poem," Boston, 1764; "The American War, a Poem," and other works.

The Conquest of Canada; or, The Siege of Quebec. An Historical Tragedy of Five Acts. 8vo, pp v.–76. *London:* Printed for the Author, 1766. Another Edition, 12mo, *Philadelphia*, 1772.

COLMAN, BENJAMIN.

BENJAMIN COLMAN, born in Boston, October 19, 1673; died there, 1747, was graduated from Harvard in 1692, and entered the pulpit in the following year at Medford, Mass. On a voyage to England in 1695 his vessel was attacked by a French privateer. He fought with the crew, and was taken with them and confined in France as a prisoner of war. He was finally exchanged and enabled to go to London. He preached there several times, and was urged to remain, but was called in 1699 to be the first minister of the Brattle Street Church in Boston, where he officiated until his death. He was made D.D. by the University of Glasgow in 1731, and in 1724 was elected President of Harvard College, but declined to serve.— *J. M.*

IN MANUSCRIPT.

Gustavus Vasa.

COOPER AND GRAY, DRS.

NOTE: These names are, with some reason, supposed to be those of the celebrated Botanist and the almost equally celebrated scientist, Dr. Cooper. They made no effort in drama except the one below mentioned.— *J. M,*

IN MANUSCRIPT.

The Renegade; or, France Restored.
Played at the Park Theatre, September 26, 1822.

CRAFTS, WILLIAM.

WILLIAM CRAFTS, born in Charleston, S. C., January 24, 1787; died in Lebanon Springs, N. Y., September 23, 1826. He was educated at Harvard and was especially noted there for his proficiency in the classic languages. He returned to Charleston, where he was admitted to the bar, and became a leading lawyer and legislator. He was always a ready and convincing speaker. In 1817 he delivered the Phi Beta Kappa address at Harvard. He was a constant contributor to the " Charleston Courier." His works were published in Charleston in 1828. He wrote a few volumes of poetry, viz.: " The Raciad," " Sullivan's Island," and " A Monody on the Death of Decatur."

The Sea Serpent; or, Gloucester Hoax. A Dramatic Jeu d'Esprit, in Three Acts.
12mo, pp 34.   *Charleston:* A. E. MILLER, 1819.

CROSWELL, JOSEPH.

A New World Planted; or, the Adventures of the Forefathers of New England Who Landed in Plymouth, December 22, 1620. An Historical Drama.
8vo, pp 45.   *Boston,* 1802.

CUSTIS, GEORGE WASHINGTON PARKE.

George Washington Parke Custis, born in Mount Airy, Md., April 30, 1786; died at Arlington, Fairfax Co., Va., October 10, 1857. His father was the son of Mrs. Washington by her former husband. His early home was at Mount Vernon, and he was educated at Princeton. He married, early in life, Mary Lee Fitzhugh, and their daughter married Robert E. Lee. Arlington House, built by Mr. Custis, thus came into the Lee family. This beautiful estate, which was confiscated during the war between the States, and used as a place of burial for the Federal dead, was purchased from General Lee's heirs at the close of the war and remains dedicated to the uses of a National Cemetery. Mr. Custis wrote " Recollections of General Washington," published first in the " National Intelligencer," and in book form in New York, in 1860.— *J. M.*

Pocahontas; or, The Settlers of Virginia. A National Drama in Three Acts.

12mo, pp 47. *Philadelphia*, 1830.

Another Edition. 12mo, pp 45. *Philadelphia*, 1839.

This play was first acted at the Park Theatre, New York, December 28, 1830, was well received, and was played in different cities of the United States.

(DA PONTE, *so called*), *properly :* —
DA CENEDA, LORENZO DA PONTE.

Lorenzo Da Ponte Da Ceneda; born in Venice, Italy, in 1748; died in New York, August 17, 1838,

was an ardent poet and dramatist, and was attached
to the Court Theatre at Vienna in 1784, where several
of his librettos were produced with success. He came
to New York about 1809, and established himself as a
teacher of languages, finally becoming Professor of
Italian Literature in Columbia College. He was a
very popular figure in New York society, and dearly
loved by his compatriots, to whom he gave an affectionate welcome upon their coming to his new home.
He was an intimate associate of Mozart, Metastasio,
and Joseph II. of Austria. Upon the arrival of the
first Italian opera of Signor Garcia and his illustrious
daughter in New York, they found that Da Ponte had
made their way to triumph easy. He was, in fact,
the foster-father of Italian opera in America.— *J. M.*

Assur Re d'Ormus.   Dramma.

     18mo, pp 47.   *New York:* STAMPATORI GIOVANNI
GRAY E CIA, 1826.

Il Don Giovanni.   Dramma Eroicomica.

     18mo, pp 51.   *Nova-Jorca:* STAMPATORI GIOVANNI
GRAY E CIA, 1826.

Le Nozze di Figaro.   Dramma Eroicomica.

     18mo, pp iv. 3–63.   *New York,* STAMPATORI GIOVANNI
GRAY E CIA, 1826.

**Le Nozze di Figaro, Il Don Giovanni, e
L'Assur Re d'Ormus.**   Tre Drammi.

     18mo, pp (2) ii, iv. 3–63, 51, 47.   [*New York*], STAMPA-
TORI GIOVANNI GRAY E CIA, 1826.

L'Ape Musicale.   Azione Teatrale in un atto; Da
Rappresentari Nel Teatro Del Park, A New York,
Per La Prima Volta.

16mo, pp 37.   *New York*, STAMPATORI DA G. F. BUNCE, 1830.

Played at the Park Theatre, New York, by the Italian Opera Company, April 20, 1830.

IN MANUSCRIPT.

The Italian Husband.   A Tragedy.

The Roman Wife.   A Tragedy.

DA PONTE, LORENZO L.

LORENZO L. DA PONTE was the son of the last-named author, and was Professor of Italian Literature and Language in the University of the City of New York up to the time of his death in 1840.   He published a " History of Florence," and " Memorie di Lorenzo Da Ponte da Cenada," 3 vols., New York, 1823.— *J. M.*

Almachide.   A Tragedy.
12mo, *New York*, 1830.

DARLING, DAVID.

Beaux Without Belles.   A Farce.
Played in Petersburg, Va.

DEERING, NATHANIEL.

NATHANIEL DEERING, born June 25, 1791; died near Portland, Me., in 1881.   His grandfather, of the same name, was one of the founders of that city.   The subject of this memoir began his education at Phillips Academy, Exeter, and was graduated from Harvard College in 1810. He was admitted to the Bar in 1815, and practiced for a time in Canaan and Milburn (now Skowhegan), Maine. He removed to Portland in 1836, and devoted himself to literature. He was the first editor of the " Independent Statesman."

J. M.

Carrabasset; or, The Last of the Norridge-wocks. A Tragedy in Two Acts.
18mo, pp 54. *Portland*, 1830.

DEFFENBACH, F.

Onliata; or, The Indian Heroine.
12mo, *Philadelphia*, 1821.

D'ELVILLE, RINALLO.

The Rescue; or, The Villain Unmasked. A Farce in Three Acts.
12mo, pp 44. *New York:* Printed for the author, 1813.

IN MANUSCRIPT.

Clairvoyants. A Comedy.
Played in Boston.

DODDRIDGE, JOSEPH.

DR. JOSEPH DODDRIDGE, born in Pennsylvania in 1769; died in Wellsburg, Brooke County, Va., in

November, 1826. He was educated at Jefferson
Academy, Canonsburg, Pa., and ordained to the min-
istry in the Protestant Episcopal Church in 1792.
He is well known as the author of " A History of the
Indian Wars," considered the best book on that sub-
ject.— *J. M.*

**Logan, The Last of the Race of Skikellemus,
Chief of the Cayuga Nation.** A Dramatic
Piece. To which is added, the Dialogue of The
Backwoodsman and the Dandy, First recited at
the Buffaloe Seminary, July the 1st, 1821, by Dr.
Joseph Doddridge.

12mo, pp 47. *Buffalo Creek, Brooke County, Va.:* Printed
for the Author, by SOLOMON SALA, at the Buffaloe Printing
Office, 1823.

Reprinted in 4to size, pp 76. *Cincinnati,* 1868.

DUMONT, J. B.

IN MANUSCRIPT.

The Invisible Witness.
Played in 1824.

DUNLAP, WILLIAM.

WILLIAM DUNLAP, rightly called the father of the
American Stage, was born in Perth Amboy, N. J.,
February 19, 1766, and died in New York, September 28, 1839. He came to New York in 1777 and
commenced the study of painting, for which he had

an early inclination. In 1784 he went to London, where for three years he worked under Benjamin West. On his return he became interested in the drama, and wrote his first play. He soon after became closely identified with the theatre, and appeared on the stage. In 1796 he became manager of the John Street Theatre, and, soon after, sole manager of the New Park Theatre. In 1805 he retired from the management a bankrupt, and devoted himself to his original profession of painting. In 1814 he received the appointment of Assistant Paymaster General of the New York State Militia. In 1817 he again took up the brush, and exhibited some of his large paintings in most of the cities of the United States. He was founder and vice-president of the National Academy of Design. He wrote " The Life of George Frederick Cooke," and " A History of the Rise and Progress of the Art of Design in America "—a most valuable work. He also wrote a number of other works on different subjects.

The Father; or, American Shandyism. A Comedy in Five Acts, as performed at the New York Theatre by the old American Company, September 7, 1789. Written by a citizen of New York.

> 8vo, pp 68. *New York,* 1789.
> Dunlap's first published play.
> Reprinted by the Dunlap Society, 1887.

Darby's Return. A Comic Sketch, as performed at the New York Theatre, November 24, 1789, For the Benefit of Mr. Wignell.

8vo, pp 16. *New York:* Printed by HODGE, ALLEN, AND CAMPBELL, and sold at their respective Bookstores, and by BERRY and ROGERS, 1789.

Sequel to "The Poor Soldier."

Another Edition. 12mo, *New York*, 1806.

Also reprinted in the Appendix to "Washington and the Theatre," by Paul L. Ford, New York, 1899.

The Archers; or, Mountaineers of Switzerland. An Opera in Three Acts, as performed by the Old American Co. in New York.

8vo, pp 94. *New York*, 1796.

Played at the Park Theatre, New York, April 18, 1796.

Tell Truth and Shame the Devil! A Farce.

12mo, pp 44. *New York*, 1797.

Played at the John Street Theatre, January 9, 1797.

The Knight's Adventure. A Comedy.

12mo, *New York*, 1797.

A play was announced to be played at the John Street Theatre, in 1797, under the title of "The Man of Fortitude; or, The Knight's Adventure," by Jno. Hodgkinson [q. v.], and Dunlap asserts that it was taken bodily from his play while the Ms. was in Hodgkinson's hands.

André. A Tragedy in Five Acts, as performed by the Old American Co., New York, March 30th, 1798. To which are added authentic documents respecting Major André; Consisting of letters to Miss Seward, the Cow Chase, Proceedings of the Court Martial, etc.

Copyright secured.

Sm. 8vo, pp viii. 139. *New York:* Printed by T. & J. SWORDS, No. 89 Pearl Street, 1798.

Another Edition. 8vo, *London*, 1799.
Reprinted by the Dunlap Society.
First produced at the New Park Theatre, New York, March 30, 1798.

The Stranger. A Tragedy.

12mo, *New York*, 1798.
Adapted from the German of Kotzebue.
Played at the John Street Theatre, New York, December 10, 1798.
Probably this is a reprint of the English translation.

False Shame; or, The American Orphan in Germany. A Comedy, from the German of A. Von Kotzebue.

12mo, pp 76. *New York*, 1800.
Another Edition. 12mo, pp 76. *Charleston*, 1800.
Played at the Park Theatre, New York, December 11, 1799.

Virgin of the Sun. A Drama, from the German of A. Von Kotzebue.

12mo, *New York*, 1800.
Played at the Park Theatre, New York, March 12, 1800.

The Wild Goose Chase. A Play in Four Acts, with songs.

12mo, *New York*, 1800.
Played at the Park Theatre, New York, January 24, 1800.

Pizarro in Peru; or, The Death of Rolla. A Play in Five Acts, from the German of Aug. Von Kotzebue.

8vo, *New York*, 1800.
Played at the Park Theatre, New York, March 26, 1800.

Abaellino, The Great Bandit. A Grand Dramatic Romance, from Zschokke, in Five Acts.

5

12mo, *Boston* and *New York*, 1802.
Another Edition.　*New York*, 1803.
Played at the Park Theatre, New York, February 11, 1801.

The Glory of Columbia, her Yeomanry. A Comedy.

12mo, pp 12.　*New York*, 1803.
Another Edition.　18mo, pp 56.　*New York*, 1817.
This is the play of "André" entirely rewritten.
Played at the Park Theatre, New York, July 4, 1803.

Ribbemont; or, The Feudal Baron. A Tragedy.

18mo, pp 72.　*New York*, 1803.
Played at the John Street Theatre, New York, October 31, 1776, under the title of "The Mysterious Monk."

Blue Beard; or, Female Curiosity. A Dramatic Romance in Three Acts.

18mo, pp 48.　*New York*, 1803.
Another Edition.　16mo.　*New York*, 1806.

The Voice of Nature. A Drama in Three Acts, as performed at the New York Theatre.

18mo, pp 41.　*New York*, 1803.
From the French play, "Le Jugement de Saloman."
Played at the Park Theatre, New York, February 4, 1803.

The Fatal Deception; or, The Progress of Guilt.

Performed at the Park Theatre, New York, April 24, 1794.
Published as

Lord Leicester. A Tragedy.

16mo, pp 150.　*New York*, 1807.

Fountainville Abbey. A Tragedy.

18mo, pp 211.　*New York*, 1807.
From Mrs. Radcliff's "Romance of the Forest."
Played at the John Street Theatre, New York, February 16, 1795.

The Father of an Only Child. A Comedy.
> 18mo, pp 81. *New York,* 1807.
> This is the play of "The Father," with a new title.

The Blind Boy. A Comedy, altered from Kotzebue's Epigram.
> 12mo, *New York,* 1808.
> Played at the Park Theatre, New York, March 30, 1802.

Fraternal Discord. A Comedy. Altered from
(Kotzebue's "Bruders Twist") the German.
> 18mo, pp 67. *New York,* 1809.
> Played at the Park Theatre, New York, October 24, 1800.

The Italian Father. A Comedy in Five Acts.
> 18mo, pp 63. *New York,* 1810.
> Played at the New Park Theatre, New York, April 15,
> 1799.

Rinaldo Rinaldini; or, The Great Banditti.
A Tragedy. By an American and a Citizen of
New York.
> 18mo, pp 82. *New York,* 1810. Frontispiece.
> Played at the Park Theatre, New York, 1810.

Wife of Two Husbands. A Drama in Five Acts,
interspersed with Songs, Choruses, Music and
Dances.
> 18mo, pp 55. *New York,* 1811.
> Played at the Park Theatre, New York, April 4, 1804.

**Yankee Chronology; or, Huzza for the Con-
stitution.** A Musical Interlude, in One Act, to
which are added, The Patriotic Songs of the Freedom of the Seas, and Yankee Tars.
> 16mo, pp 16. *New York,* 1812.
> Played at the Park Theatre, New York, 1812.

Peter the Great; or, the Russian Mother. A Play in Five Acts.

> 18mo, pp 56. *New York*, 1814.
> Played at the Park Theatre, New York, November 15, 1801.

The Good Neighbor. An Interlude in One Act, as performed at the New York Theatre, February 28, 1803.

> 18mo, pp 12. *New York*, 1814.

The Wreck of Honor; or, Adventures in Paris. A Tragedy. Translated from the French.

> 16mo, pp 87. *New York*, 1828.

A Trip to Niagara; or, Travellers in America. A Farce in Three Acts.

> 18mo, pp 54. *New York*, 1830.
> Dunlap's last published play.
> Played at the New Bowery Theatre, New York, October 28, 1829.

IN MANUSCRIPT.

The Modest Soldier; or, Love in New York. (Never acted.)

The Wedding. A Comedy.

> Played at the John Street Theatre, New York, May 20, 1793.

Shelty's Travels. A Farce. Sequel to " The Highland Reel."

> Played at the John Street Theatre, New York, April 24, 1794.

Sterne's Maria; or, The Vintage. An Opera.

> Played at the Park Theatre, New York, January 11, 1799.

The Natural Daughter. A Comedy.
> Played at the Park Theatre, New York, February 8, 1799.

The Temple of Independence. A Pageant in honor of Washington's Birthday.
> Played at the Park Theatre, New York, February 22, 1799.

The Stranger. A translation from Kotzebue's "Menschenhass und Reue."
> Played at the Park Theatre, New York, December 10, 1798.

Love's Vows. A Comedy. Translated from Kotzebue's "Natural Son."
> Played at the Park Theatre, New York, March 11, 1799.
> An edition in 12mo, pp 74, *New York*, 1814, of this play was probably the reprint of a version made in England. Dunlap says ("History of the American Theatre," vol. ii, p. 95) that his translation was not published.

Count Benyowski. A translation from Kotzebue's drama of the same name.
> Played at the Park Theatre, New York, April 1, 1799.

Don Carlos. A translation from Schiller's drama of the same name.
> Played at the Park Theatre, New York, May 6, 1799.

The School for Soldiers. A translation from the French drama "The Deserter."
> Played at the Park Theatre, New York, July 4, 1799.

The Force of Calumny. A translation from Kotzebue's comedy of the same name.
> Played at the Park Theatre, New York, February 5, 1800.

The Robbery. A translation from the French.
> Played at the Park Theatre, December 30, 1799.

The Knight of Guadalquiver.   An Opera.
> Played at the Park Theatre, New York, December 5, 1800.

The Count of Burgundy.   A translation from Kotzebue.
> Played at the Park Theatre, New York, March 3, 1800.

The Corsicans; or, The Dawnings of Love.
> Played at the Park Theatre, New York, April 21, 1800.

Abbé de l'Epée.   From the French.
> Played at the Park Theatre, New York, April, 1801.

Where Is He?   A Farce.   From the German.
> Played at the Park Theatre, New York, December 4, 1801.

The Retrospect.   A Patriotic Pageant.
> Played at the Park Theatre, New York, Monday, July 5, 1802.

Bonaparte in England.   A Farce.
> Played at the Park Theatre, New York, December 19, 1803.

The Proverb; or, Conceit Can Cure, Conceit Can Kill.   A Comedy.
> Played at the Park Theatre, New York, February 21, 1804.

Lewis of Monte Blanco; or, the Transplanted Irishman.   A Comedy.
> Played at the Park Theatre, New York, March 12, 1804.

Thirty Years; or, the Life of a Gamester. From the French.
> Played at the New Bowery Theatre, New York, February 20, 1828.

It Is a Lie!   A Farce.
> Played at the New Bowery Theatre, New York, August 20, 1828.

Self Immolation; or Family Distress. From the German of Kotzebue.

> Played at the Park Theatre, New York, November 29, 1799.

The Stranger's Birthday. Sequel to "The Stranger." A Dramatic Sketch.

> Played at the Park Theatre, New York, April 23, 1800.

The Indians in England; or Nabob of Mysore. From the German of Kotzebue.

> Played at the Park Theatre, June 14, 1799.

Battle of New Orleans.

> Played at the Park Theatre, New York, July 4, 1815.

Nina. An Operetta.

> Played at the Grove Theatre, in Bedlow Street, New York, December 28, 1804.

The Miser's Wedding.

The Soldier of '76.

La Perouse.

The Merry Gardener.

Forty and Twenty.

Robespierre.

The Flying Dutchman.

> NOTE. Dunlap says he was accustomed to lend his plays in MS. to different managers, and in that way many of them were lost. See note under CHARLES SMITH *post*.

EATON, N. W.

Alberto and Matilda. A Drama.
18mo, pp 17. *Boston*, 1809.

ELLIOT, SAMUEL.

Fayette in Prison; or, Misfortunes of the Great. A Modern Tragedy by a Gentleman of Boston.
8vo, pp 40. *Worcester*, Printed for the Author. 1800.
Reprinted with this change in title, "by a Gentleman of Massachusetts," 8vo, pp 40. *Worcester*, Is. THOMAS, 1802.

ELLIS, MRS.

IN MANUSCRIPT.

The Duke of Buckingham.
Played at the Park Theatre, New York, June 21, 1809.

ELLISON, JAMES.

IN MANUSCRIPT.

The American Captives; or, the Siege of Tripoli.
Played in Boston in 1812.

EUSTAPHIEVE, ALEXIS.

Alexis, the Czarewitz. A Tragedy in 5 Acts. This play was published in a volume of poems entitled, Reflections, Notes, and Original Anecdotes, illustrating the Character of Peter the Great.
12mo, pp 272. *Boston*, 1814.

EVANS, NATHANIEL.

NATHANIEL EVANS, born in Philadelphia, Penn., June 8, 1742; died in Gloucester County, N. J., October 29, 1767, was graduated from the College of Philadelphia, and ordained in England by the Bishop of London. As a member of the British Society for the Propagation of the Gospel in Foreign Parts, he settled in Gloucester County, N. J., and became noted for his eloquence as a preacher. He wrote some very graceful verses, which were collected and published after his death as " Poems on Several Occasions " (1772).—*J. M.*

An Exercise, Containing a Dialogue and Ode on Peace. Performed at the Public Commencement in the College of Philadelphia, May 17th, 1763.

     8vo, pp. 8. *Philadelphia:* Printed by ANDREW STEWART, 1763.

     The Ode was written by Dr. Paul Jackson, of Chester, Pennsylvania.

EVERETT, DAVID.

DAVID EVERETT, born in Princeton, Mass., March 29, 1770; died in Marietta, Ohio, December 21, 1813, was graduated from Dartmouth in 1795. Before entering College he taught School at New Ipswich, studied law in Boston, and wrote for " Russell's Gazette and Farmer's Museum," in which his prose papers " Common Sense in Deshabille," became quite popular. They were published in a volume in

6

1799. He also contributed to a literary paper called "The Nightingale" in 1796. In 1809 he edited the "Boston Patriot," and in 1812 "The Pilot," a paper in the interest of De Witt Clinton for the Presidency. He left Boston in 1813 for Marietta, Ohio, with the purpose of establishing a newspaper there, but death interrupted his plans.

Daranzel; or, the Persian Patriot. An original Drama in Five Acts; as performed at the Theatre in Boston; by David Everett, corrected and improved by a literary friend.

     8vo, pp 68. *Boston*, JOHN RUSSELL, 1800.

EWING, ROBERT W.

IN MANUSCRIPT.

Le Solitaire.

Sponge Again.

Frontier Maid, The.

Highland Seer, The.

Election, The.

Imperial Victim, The.

La Fayette.

Quentin Durward.

Exit in a Hurry.

Bride of Death.

FAIRFIELD, SUMNER LINCOLN.

S. L. FAIRFIELD, born in Warwick, Mass., June 25, 1803; died in New Orleans, La., March 6, 1844, entered Brown University, Providence, R. I., at the age of thirteen. He studied so unremittingly, that, after a few months he was attacked with a severe sickness. On recovering he was forced to leave college and seek a living as a tutor in the Southern States. In 1825 he sailed for London and wrote his poem, "The Cities of the Plain," which appeared in the "Oriental Herald." He was received by Lafayette, in France, where he published "Pére la Chaise" and "Westminster Abbey." He returned to the United States in 1826.

Mina. A Dramatic Sketch.
12mo, pp 120. *Baltimore*, JOSEPH ROBINSON, 1825.

FAUGÉRES, MARGARETTA BLEECKER.

MARGARETTA BLEECKER FAUGÉRES, born in Tunkhannock, near Albany, New York, in 1771; died there January 9, 1801, was a daughter of the poetess Ann Eliza Bleecker. In 1791 she married Peter Faugéres, a physician of New York, who dissipated her fortune, and died in 1798. She supported herself by teaching until her death in 1801. Her poems are appended to her mother's "Posthumous Works," edited by her, New York, 1793.

Belisarius. A Tragedy.

12mo, pp 53. *New York,* 1795.

Offered to the management of the John Street Theatre and declined.

FENNELL, JAMES.

JAMES FENNELL, born in Wales in 1766; died in Philadelphia in June, 1816. He belonged to a very good family, and was given a classical education at Eton and Cambridge, and intended for the profession of the Law. He abandoned his studies in London in the year 1787, and went to Edinburgh with the intention of going upon the stage. He applied to the manager of the Theatre Royal, and made known his desire. He was given an opportunity, and under the assumed name of Chambray made an excellent impression in *Othello* and *Jaffier*. He was engaged for the season of 1788–9 under penalty of £200. He then went to London, and succeeded in so impressing Mr. Harris, the manager of Covent Garden Theatre, that he was given a special engagement, and made his appearance there as *Othello*. Received with much approbation, he was offered a London engagement and payment of his £200 penalty; but refused, and went back to Edinburgh where, on account of his success in the part of *Jaffier*, a cabal was made against him by Mr. Wood, who had been the leading man of the theatre. He left Edinburgh after a year of quarreling, and was engaged at Covent Garden for the season of 1789.

He came to America in 1794, and made his first appearance in Philadelphia, where he remained, for some years, a great favorite both on and off the stage. He first played in New York at the Park Theatre as *Zanga* in "The Revenge," September 8, 1800. He retired from the stage in 1814, and engaged in the business of making salt from sea water, near New London, Conn. His last years were spent in poverty and dissipation — a sad example of wasted opportunities. His autobiography was published in 1814.

J. M.

IN MANUSCRIPT.

The Wheel of Truth.   A Farce.
    Played at the Park Theatre, New York, January 12, 1803.

Lindor and Clari.

Picture of Paris.

FIELD, ——.

France and Liberty.

Rhyme Without Reason.   A Farce.

FINN, HENRY JAMES.

HENRY JAMES FINN, born in Cape Breton in 1785; died on the steamer *Lexington* off Eaton's Neck, Long Island Sound, January 13, 1840, was the son of an officer in the English navy, who retired from that service, and settled with his family in New York when

Finn was a mere child. His early education was received at the Academy at Hackensack, and he was for a time a student at Princeton. While a copying clerk in the office of Mr. Thomas Phoenix, in New York City, he found means to become a supernumerary in the Park Theatre, and, having a taste for drawing, took much interest in scene painting. On the death of his father he was taken to England by his mother, and there was subjected to such privation that he gladly took a place in a company of country players. He was finally engaged at the Haymarket, London, where he first appeared, May 15, 1811, as *Lopez* in "The Honeymoon," and for two seasons was an important member of the company. In 1818 he went to Savannah, where he played successfully for a year, and in 1820 became associated with J. K. Tefft as editor and publisher of "The Georgian," a daily newspaper. In 1821 he went again to England, and, besides playing with success, made material reputation, and profit as a miniature painter. He returned to America, and made a brilliant success as *Richard III* at the Federal Street Theatre, Boston, October 28, 1822. From that time, to his tragic death on the loss of the *Lexington* by fire, he was a very popular actor of tragedy and light comedy.— *J. M.*

Montgomery ; or, the Falls of Montmorency.
A Drama in Three Acts, as acted at the Boston Theatre.

12mo. pp 11, 56. *Boston*, 1825.
This play was acted with much success.

FOOT, JOHN FORESTER.

The Little Thief; or, the Night Walker.

FORREST, COLONEL THOMAS.
(See BARTON, ANDREW.)

Disenchantment (Disappointment); or, the Force of Credulity. A New American Comic Opera of Three Acts, by Andrew Barton, Esquire.
New York, 1767.

"Perhaps an assumed name for Colonel Thomas Forrest, of Germantown," a MS. note on an old copy in the Library of Philadelphia. This opera was rehearsed by the Douglas Company in Philadelphia, but was withdrawn, supposedly on account of personal allusions of a rather pointed character.

J. M.

FOSTER, ——.

The Inheritance.

FOWLER, MANLY B.

The Prophecy; or, Love and Friendship. A Drama.
18mo, pp 34. *New York,* 1821.

FRISBIE, NOAH, JR.

NOAH FRISBIE, JR., born in Woodbury, Conn., Jan. 23, 1758, was the oldest son of Noah Frisbie of the same town who married Margery Post in 1752, and was in 1757 a member of Captain Ebenezer Downs' company of volunters in the expedition for the relief of Fort William Henry on Lake George against the French. On the "Alarm of Lexington," Noah Frisbie with his two sons Noah and Jonathan, and their kinsmen Asabel, Abiel, David and James, joined the Continental forces. Noah Frisbie, Jr., appears on the army list at the end of the war as a Lieutenant. No futher information, except the printing of the under-mentioned play, is available.—*J. M.*

GODFREY, THOMAS, Jr.

Thomas Godfrey, who was born in Philadelphia on December 4, 1736, and died near Wilmington, N. C., August 3, 1763, was a son of Thomas Godfrey, the inventor of the quadrant. He was apprenticed to a watchmaker and remained at that trade until 1758. He was an officer in the expedition against Fort Du Quesne. He removed to North Carolina and remained there three years. He then went to Philadelphia and sailed as a supercargo to the Island of New Providence, returning from thence to North Carolina, where a few weeks after his arrival, by exposure to the sun on horseback, he contracted a fever which terminated fatally.

Juvenile Poems on Various Subjects, and Prince of Parthia, A Tragedy.

8vo, pp XVI, 223. *Philadelphia.* Printed by HENRY MILLER, in Second Street, 1765.

The Prince of Parthia is the earliest known tragedy that was written by an American. The play was offered to the company then performing in Philadelphia, but was not accepted.

GRICE, C. E.

IN MANUSCRIPT.

The Battle of New Orleans.

Played at the Park Theatre, New York, July 4, 1816.

HALL, EVERARD.

Nolens Volens; or, the Biter Bit.

HAMILTON, COLONEL.

The Enterprise. An Opera.

Played in Baltimore, 1823.

HARBY, ISAAC.

ISAAC HARBY, born in Charleston, S. C., November 9, 1788; died in New York City, November 14, 1828, first studied Law under Langdon Cheves, but soon gave this up to become the principal of a school on Edisto Island. His first literary work was the editing of a weekly paper called "The Quiver." This paper had but a short existence, and he purchased "The Investigator," which he changed to "The Southern Patriot." In 1822 he conducted "The City Gazette," and wrote for "The Charleston Mercury."

7

The second representation of " Alberti," in Charleston, 1819, was honored by the presence of President Monroe. "Alberti" was written for Cooper, but he never appeared in the character. Harby is said to have been the finest dramatic critic of his time in America. He came to New York in 1828.

Alberti. A Play.

> 12mo, pp 55.   *Charleston,* 1819.
> Republished with a selection of his writings.   *Charleston,* 1829.
> This play was performed at the Charleston Theatre, 1818.

HATTON, ANN JULIA.

ANN JULIA HATTON was a member of the Kemble family and a sister of Mrs. Siddons. She was the wife of Wm. Hatton, a celebrated musical instrument maker, at No. 3 Peck Slip, New York City.

The Songs of Tammany ; or, the Indian Chief. A Serious Opera, by Ann Julia Hatton. To be had at the printing-office of John Harrisson, No. 3 Peck Slip, and of Mr. Faulkner, at the Box-Office of the Theatre.   [Price one shilling.]

> 16mo, pp 16.   *New York,* 1794.
> The Opera from which these songs were taken (Tammany ; or, The Indian Chief), was written for the Tammany Society, and was first played at the John Street Theatre March 3, 1794, and "had a great run."
> No trace can be found of the play itself being published.
> The Prologue to Tammany was published in a volume of poems by R. B. DAVIS.   *New York,* 1807, pp 120–1.

IN MANUSCRIPT.

Tammany. An opera.

> Acted at the John Street Theatre, New York, March 3, 1794.

HAWKINS, MICAH.

The Saw Mill; or, A Yankee Trick. A Comic Opera.

> 12mo, *New York*, 1824.
>
> Played at the Park Theatre, New York, November 29, 1825.

HENRY, JOHN.

JOHN HENRY was a native of Dublin, and made his début at Drury Lane, in 1762, with little success. He joined Douglas's Company in the West Indies, and coming to New York from there made his first appearance on the American stage at the John Street Theatre, New York, December 7, 1767, playing in America until the close of the year 1794.

He died in 1795, on a vessel bound for Newport.

"It is recorded that for many years after the Revolution, Mr. Henry was the only actor in New York who kept a coach, and that in his case frequent attacks of the gout rendered it a necessity." The panels of the coach were decorated with a representation of two crutches crossed, and the motto, "This or These."

A School for Soldiers; or, The Deserter. A Dramatic Poem.

> 8vo. Printed at Kingston in Jamaica (W. I.) 1783.
>
> This piece was first played in Kingston.
>
> Played at the John Street Theatre, New York, April 24, 1788.

IN MANUSCRIPT.

The Convention; or, The Columbian Father.
A Pageant.
> Played at the John Street Theatre, April 7, 1787.

Orvidus; or, The Columbian Father. A Serious Dramatic Pastoral.
> *New York*, 1786.
> Altered and revised and called ——

The Convention; or, The Columbian Father,
in 1788.
> Autograph Ms. in library of " The Players," N. Y.

The American Soldier. A Comedy.
> Autograph Ms. in library of " The Players," N. Y.

True Blue; or, The Sailor's Festival. A Farce.
> Autograph Ms. in library of " The Players," N. Y.

HILLHOUSE, JAMES ABRAHAM.

JAMES ABRAHAM HILLHOUSE, born in New Haven, September 26, 1789; died there January 5, 1841, son of Hon. James Hillhouse, was graduated from Yale in 1808, came to New York and engaged in business as a merchant, but soon retired, and gave his time to literary pursuits.

Percy's Masque. A Drama in Five Acts, from the London Edition.
> 12mo, *New York*, 1820.
> It is doubtful if a London edition of this piece was published.

Hadad. A Dramatic Poem, by James A. Hillhouse, author of " Percy's Masque " and " The Judgment."
> 8vo, pp 208. *New York*, 1825.

Demetria. A Domestic Tragedy in Five Acts.

This piece was written in 1813, but was not published until 1839, when it was included in the "Works" of the author. 2 vols., *Boston*, 1839.

HITCHCOCK, EDWARD.

EDWARD HITCHCOCK, born in Deerfield, Mass., May 24, 1793; died in Amherst, Mass., February 27, 1864. In 1816 he became principal of the Academy in Deerfield, where he remained for three years. He was ordained minister of the Congregational Church at Conway, Mass., in 1821. In 1825 he was appointed Professor of Chemistry and Natural History in Amherst College. He continued his connection with the College, having been appointed to the presidency with the professorship of Natural Theology and Geology, until his resignation in 1854. He was the author of numerous scientific and theological works. The tragedy mentioned below is his first and probably his only dramatic production. He died in 1864.

The Downfall of Buonaparte. A Tragedy.

8vo, pp 108. *Deerfield*, 1815 (?)

HODGKINSON, JOHN.

JOHN HODGKINSON was born in Manchester, Eng., in 1767; died in Washington, D. C., December 12, 1805. His real name was Meadowcraft. His first successes were on the Bath stage. He came to America with the company of Hallam & Henry, and made his début at the John Street Theatre in 1793.

He bought out Henry's interest, and continued one of the managers until 1798. He went to Charleston, S. C., in 1803, but became a victim of yellow fever while travelling, and died near Washington, D. C.

The Man of Fortitude; or, The Knight's Adventure. A Drama in Three Acts.

12mo, pp 32. *New York*, 1807.

Played at the John Street Theatre, New York, June 7, 1797.

Dunlap says that this play was rewritten in prose upon the text of a manuscript in blank verse in one act called " The Knight's Adventure," which Dunlap had submitted to Hodgkinson some years previously and declares that the latter seemed unconscious of any wrong-doing.

Robin Hood.

12mo. *New York*, 1808.

HOLLAND, EDWIN CLIFFORD.

Edwin Clifford Holland, born in Charleston, S. C., in 1794; died there September 11, 1824. He was editor of the " Charleston Times," and author of "Odes, Naval Songs, etc." Charleston, 1814.—*J. M.*

The Corsair. A Drama.

HOPKINSON, FRANCIS.

Francis Hopkinson, born in Philadelphia, Pa., September 21, 1737; died there May 9, 1791, was the son of Thomas Hopkinson. Francis was educated at the College of Philadelphia, studied law under

Benjamin Chew, and was admitted to the bar in 1761.
His career belongs to the public history of the making
of the United States. To enumerate his works and
honors would transcend the scope of this book. He
was a member of the Continental Congress in 1776,
signed the Declaration of Independence, and was the
first head of the treasury department of the new government. The first powerful satire of the British in
Revolution, "The Battle of the Kegs," was from his
pen. A ripe scholar and a prolific writer of prose and
verse in both humorous and earnest methods, skilled
in music and in polite conversation, he was one of the
most brilliant of the group of early jurists and writers
of our country. He was United States District Judge
of Pennsylvania at the time of his death. The authorship of the two college dialogues cited below is posi-
tively given to him in the Brinley Catalogue (New
York, March, 1880), in view of which, and of the not
less important fact that Thomas Hopkinson died in
1751, I think, notwithstanding the statement made by
a contemporary newspaper, that the Dialogue of the
1766 commencement was his work. Of that occasion
Sanderson's "Biography of the Signers of the Declaration of Independence" says in the memoir of Francis
Hopkinson:

"Among the records of a public commencement of
that institution" (the College of Philadelphia), "held
on the twentieth of May, 1766, the board of trustees,
comprising the governor, chief justice and most distinguished men of the province, passed the following

resolution: ' After the business of the commencement
was finished it was resolved that as Francis Hopkinson (who was the first scholar entered in this seminary
at its opening and likewise one of the first who received a degree in it) was about to embark for
England and has always done honor to the place of
his education by his abilities and good morals, as well
as rendered it many substantial services on all public
occasions, the thanks of this institution ought to be
delivered to him in the most affectionate manner.' "

**An Exercise, Containing a Dialogue and Ode
on the Accession of His present Gracious
Majesty, George III.** Performed at the Public
Commencement in the College of Philadelphia,
May 18th, 1762.

    4to, pp 8. *Philadelphia:* Printed by W. DUNLAP, 1762.

Dialogue [in verse] **for the Commencement** in
the College of Philadelphia, May 30th, 1765.

    8vo, pp 4, 1765.

HOPKINSON, THOMAS.

THOMAS HOPKINSON, born in London, England,
April 6, 1709; died in Philadelphia, Pa., November 5,
1751, was son of a London merchant. In 1731,
having been admitted to the bar, he settled in Philadelphia, where he became a deputy, and finally principal clerk of the Orphan's Court. For many years
he was a member of the council of the province and a

judge of court. Always interested in letters and science, he became the intimate friend of Franklin, to whom he suggested the use of metal points for the purpose of obtaining electric sparks. The Library Company, the College of Philadelphia, and the Philosophical Society named him among their incorporators and earliest officers. Perhaps his greatest distinction is now that he was the father of Francis Hopkinson, who may have caused the under-mentioned dialogue to be produced " for remembrance."— *J. M.*

An Exercise, Containing a Dialogue and Two Odes. Performed at the Public Commencement in the College of Philadelphia, May 20th, 1766.

    Sm. 4to, pp 8.   *Philadelphia:* Printed by W. DUNLAP, 1766.

    The *Pennsylvania Journal* of June 5, 1766, is authority for the authorship of this exercise.

HOSMER, WM. H. C.

WILLIAM HENRY CUYLER HOSMER was born at Avon, in the valley of the Genesee, New York, May 25, 1814, and died there May 23, 1877. He was graduated from the University of Vermont, and was for many years a well-known lawyer and writer on the subjects of North American Indians, and their lore. He contributed a number of articles to magazines, and also published several volumes of poetry. His poetical works were published in two volumes in 1854, when the author was a clerk in the Custom House of the port of New York.

8

The Fall of Tecumseh.   A Drama.

12mo.   *Avon*, 1830.

This play, written when the author was but sixteen years of age, was his first literary work.

HUMPHREYS, DAVID.

DAVID HUMPHREYS was born in Derby, Conn., in July, 1753; died in New Haven, Conn., February 21, 1818. He was graduated from Yale College in 1767, and at the beginning of the Revolution entered the army. In 1778 he was attached to the staff of General Putnam, with the rank of Major.

In 1780 he was made a Colonel and aide-de-camp to Washington. He was custodian of the standards surrendered at Yorktown and was presented with a sword by Congress.

In 1784 he was appointed Secretary to the Legation for concluding treaties with foreign powers.

He resided at Mount Vernon until the framing of the Constitution, when he came to New York with the President.

In 1790 he was nominated Ambassador to Portugal, and sailed for that country in 1791. He was afterwards appointed to represent the United States at Madrid, and during this time concluded treaties of peace with Tripoli and Algiers. He was the author of a number of works, including a Life of General Israel Putnam.

The Widow of Malabar; or, The Tyranny of Custom.   A Tragedy in Five Acts.   Translated from the French of M. Le Mierre.

8vo, pp 348. *New York*, 1790. This play was published in " The Miscellaneous Works " of Humphreys.

First played at the Philadelphia Theatre, 1790. The announcement of its performance at the John Street Theatre, New York, October 17, 1791, was in these words :

The Widow of Malabar; or, The Tyranny of Custom. A play in five acts, written by a citizen of the United States (acted at Philadelphia and Baltimore with great applause), with a prologue by J. Trumbull, LL.D.

Played at the John Street Theatre, New York, October, 1791.— *J. M.*

The Yankey in England.   A Drama in Five Acts.

12mo, pp 110, 1. N. P. N. D. (Conn. 1815.)

Dunlap says he also wrote a Comedy, and relates how he endeavored to persuade the manager, Jno. Bernard, to bring it out, but was unsuccessful. " The Yankey in England" was probably the play.

HUNTER, ROBERT.

ROBERT HUNTER was born in England, and was appointed Governor of New York in 1710. He was afterwards Governor of Jamaica, where he died in 1734.

He was the author of the celebrated letter on enthusiasm, which has been ascribed to Swift.

Androboros.   A Bographical Farce, In Three Acts, viz., The Senate, The Consistory, And The Apotheosis.   By Governour Hunter.

Printed at Monoropolis since 1st August, 1714.

The first dramatic piece published in America.

It is a severe criticism of the clergy, members, and others of Trinity Church, the principal among whom was Dr. Vesey.

The piece is excessively rare, and mentioned by few bibliographers, and then only by the first word of the title. It was published anonymously, and printed by Wm. Bradford in 1714. Only one copy is known, now in the collection of the Duke of Devonshire. A manuscript copy of it is in the collection of the late Thomas J. McKee, of New York.

The copy owned by the Duke of Devonshire formerly belonged to John Philip Kemble, the tragedian. It contains a number of manuscript corrections, probably from the hand of the author, among them the word " Bographical " on the title-page, which is changed to " Biographical " ; " Monoropolis," which is changed to " Moropolis." The title-page has been torn at the bottom, and the figures 14 appear in ink.

The following lines have been written in this copy by Kemble : —

" Androboros &c. Printed at Mosicropolis. Whoever made the correction meant, I suppose, to imply that it was printed at Μωρός Πόλις —'Fool'stown.' The corrections that run all through the piece, and the key to the characters, make me suppose that this was the author's copy."

On the Title, Kemble has written, "Collated & perfect, J. P. K. 1798."

HUTTON, JOSEPH.

JOSEPH HUTTON was born in Philadelphia, Pa., February 25, 1787, and died in Newbern, N. C., January 31, 1828. In early life he contributed verses to periodicals of that city; he also wrote prose, and published several romantic stories in a literary paper. About 1811 he published a collection of fugitive poems under the title of "Leisure Hours." He also published a poem called "The Field of Orleans," in the style of Sir Walter Scott. In 1823 he removed to

Newbern, N. C., where he established himself as a teacher and wrote for the Newbern " Sentinel."

The School for Prodigals. A Comedy in Five Acts, as performed at the New Theatre, Philadelphia.
> 18mo, pp 62. *New York*, 1809.
> Played at the Chestnut Street Theatre, Philadelphia, in 1808.

The Wounded Hussar ; or, Rightful Heir. A Musical Afterpiece in Two Acts, as performed at the New Theatre, Philadelphia.
> 18mo. *Philadelphia*, 1809.
> Played at the Chestnut Street Theatre, Philadelphia, in 1809.

Fashionable Follies. A Comedy.
> 18mo. *New York*, 1809.
> Another Edition. *Philadelphia*, 1815.

The Orphan of Prague. A Drama in Five Acts.
> 18mo. *New York*, 1810.

IN MANUSCRIPT.

Cuffee and Duffee.

Modern Honor.

HYER, W. G.

Rosa. A Melodrama in Three Acts.
> 12mo, pp 44. *New York*, 1822.

INGERSOLL, CHAS. JARED.

CHARLES JARED INGERSOLL, born in Philadelphia, Pa., October 3, 1782 ; died there May 14, 1862, was a lawyer of note, elected to Congress from Pennsylvania, 1813–15 and 1841–47. He was United States District Attorney for Pennsylvania from 1815 to 1829. He was the author of the celebrated "Inchiquin's Letters" (1810) and a "Historical Sketch of the Second War between the United States and Great Britain."

Edwy and Elgiva. A Tragedy in Five Acts. Performed at the New Theatre.

8vo, pp 84. *Philadelphia*, ASHBURY DICKINS.

Dedicated to Mrs. Merry who played Elgiva in the original production in 1801.

IN MANUSCRIPT.

Julian the Apostate.

Never played or printed.

INGHAM, JOHN.

IN MANUSCRIPT.

The Times.

The Usurper. A Tragedy.

Played in Philadelphia.

IOOR, W.

Independance; or, Which do You Like Best, The Peer or the Farmer? A Comedy.

8vo, pp 70. *Charleston*, 1805.

The Battle of the Eutaw Springs, and Evacuation of Charleston; or, the Glorious 14th of

December, 1782. A National Drama in Five Acts.

> 8vo, pp 59. *Charleston*, for the Author, 1807.
> Played in the Charleston Theatre in 1817.

JUDAH, S. B. H.

SAMUEL B. H. JUDAH was a well-known writer of New York City in the early part of the present century. He wrote a novel called " The Buccaneers," and a work entitled " Gotham and the Gothamites," both of which reflected on the society of New York at that time and caused the author to be sued for libel, and his works suppressed. His plays were performed in England as well as America.

The Mountain Torrent. A Melodrama.

> 18mo, pp v.–54. *New York*, 1820.
> Played at the Park Theatre, New York, March 1, 1820.

The Rose of Arragon; or, The Vigil of St. Mark. A Melodrama in Two Acts.

> 16mo, pp 38. *New York*, 1822.
> Played at the Park Theatre, New York, April 18, 1822.

A Tale of Lexington. A National Comedy founded on the opening of the Revolution, in Three Acts.

> 18mo, pp v.–60. *New York*, 1823.

Odofriede, the Outcast. A Dramatic Poem.

> 8vo, pp 89, (6). *New York*, 1822.

Richelieu. A Domestic Tragedy founded on Fact. (As adopted for performance at the Theatre Royal, Covent Garden, London; before it was altered by order of the Lord Chamberlain and produced under a new name.)   Now first printed from the Author's Manuscript.

18mo, *New York*, 1826.

This play has been ascribed to John Howard Payne, but the play of the same name (Richelieu) which he wrote, has a variation in the title.

KENNICOTT, JAS. H.

Irma; or, The Prediction.   A Tragedy in Five Acts, as performed at the American Theatre, New Orleans.

16mo, pp iv.–56.   *New York*, 1830.   Portrait of James H. Caldwell.

This play gained, in competition with five others, the prize of $300 offered by James H. Caldwell — the manager of the American Theatre, New Orleans.   It was played in that theatre in March, 1830.

KERR, JOHN.

Rip Van Winkle; or, The Demons of the Catskill Mountains.   A National Drama in Two Acts.

12mo, *Philadelphia*.   N. D.

Played at the Park Theatre in New York, April 22, 1830, with Mr. James H. Hackett in the title rôle.

LATHY, THOMAS PIKE.

Reparation; or, The School for Libertines.   A Drama, as performed at the Boston Theatre.

12mo, pp 46.   *Boston*, 1800.

LAWSON, JAMES.

James Lawson, born in Glasgow, Scotland, November 9, 1799; died in Yonkers, N. Y., March 20, 1880. He was educated at Glasgow University and came to New York in 1815. He was at first employed as a clerk in the counting house of a maternal uncle, who was a merchant of New York. He began writing for the New York " Literary Gazette " in 1826, and from 1827 to 1829 was the assistant editor of the " Morning Courier." He edited the " Mercantile Advertiser " from 1829 to 1833. For a time subsequently he engaged in the business of marine insurance. He published several volumes of stories and poems.— *J. M.*

Giordano. A Tragedy.
> 8vo. pp 102. *New York*, 1832.
> Played at the Park Theatre, N. Y., November 13, 1828.

LEACOCK, JOHN.

The Fall of British Tyranny ; or, American Liberty Triumphant. The First Campaign.
A Tragi-comedy of Five Acts as lately planned at the Theatrum Pandemonium at St. James. The principal place of action in America. Published according to act of Parliament.
> 8vo, pp viii.–66. *Philadelphia*, printed by Styner & Cist.
> Same 12mo, pp viii.–66. *Providence*, J. Douglas McDougall. N. D. (1776).
> Same 8vo, pp viii.–71. *Boston*, reprinted by Gill & Powars & Willis. N. D.

This is an American Chronicle Play beginning with imaginary events in England before the Revolution, showing the

9

battles about Boston and ending with the evacuation of that
city by the British. — *J. M.*

Disappointed.

12mo.   *Philadelphia*, 1796.
Played in Philadelphia, April 2, 1796.

The Medley; or, Harlequin Have at Ye All.

A Pantomime acted at Covent Garden.

8vo, 1778.

LELAND, AARON W.

AARON W. LELAND, born in Holliston, Mass., May
28, 1761; died in Chester, Vt., August 25, 1833. He
was ordained a minister of the Baptist Church about
1786, and settled in Chester, Vt. He was a member
of the Vermont Legislature from 1801 to 1811, a
councillor for four years, Lieutenant-Governor of the
State for five years, and Justice of his County Court
for eighteen years. He refused a nomination for
governor in 1828. He was a very effective orator.

J. M.

The Fatal Error.   A Tragedy.   Exhibited at Williams College, March 25, 1807.

12mo, pp 27, *Pittsfield:* Printed by SEYMOUR & SMITH,
1807.

Another edition. 12mo, pp 24. *Peterboro:* Reprinted by
JONATHAN BUNCE & Co. (Madison County), 1810.

LILLIBRIDGE, GARDNER R.

Tancred; or, The Rightful Heir to Rochdale Castle.   A Drama, altered from a tale of ancient times.

16mo, pp 68.   *Providence*, 1824.

LINDSLEY, A. B.

Love and Friendship; or, Yankee Notions.
A Comedy in Three Acts.
18mo, pp 58. *New York*, 1809.

LINN, JOHN BLAIR.

John Blair Linn was born in Shippenburg, Pa., March 24, 1777; died in Philadelphia, Pa., August 30, 1804. He was prepared for college at a boarding-school in Flushing, and entered Columbia at the age of thirteen. After his graduation he studied law with Alexander Hamilton, and during that period he wrote the play below referred to. His disposition turned towards the church, and he studied theology with Dr. Romeyn of Schenectady, and was ordained a Presbyterian minister in 1798. He then became assistant to Dr. Ewing in the First Presbyterian Church, Philadelphia. He married Hester Bailey, daughter of Col. John Bailey of Poughkeepsie, New York. The University of Pennsylvania conferred upon him the degree of D.D. in 1802. His sister married Charles Brockden Brown.—*J. M.*

IN MANUSCRIPT.

Bourville Castle; or, The Gallic Orphan.
Played at the John Street Theatre, New York, January 16, 1797.

LOW, SAMUEL.

The Politician Out-Witted. A Comedy in Five Acts, Written in 1788, By an American.
8vo, pp 71. *New York:* Printed by W. Ross, 1789.

MACPHERSON, J.

A Pennsylvania Sailor's Letters, alias, The Farmer's Fall; with Extracts from a Tragic Comedy, Called Hodge Podge Improved; or, The Race Fairly Run. The Author's Sympathy for an Innocent Woman prevents his publishing the whole of that Dramatic piece.

Number 1, 8vo, pp 64. *Philadelphia*, for the author. 1771.

MADDOCKS, ——.

The Bohemian Mother. Translated from the French.

Played in the Park Theatre, New York, April 19, 1829.

MARKOE, PETER.

PETER MARKOE, born in Santa Cruz (St. Croix), one of the West India Islands, in 1735; died in Philadelphia in 1792. He was educated at Trinity College, Dublin, read law in London, and settled in Philadelphia in 1783. He there became addicted to literature and contributed to the leading periodicals over the name "A Native of Algiers." — *J. M.*

The Patriot Chief. A Tragedy.
8vo, pp 70. *Philadelphia*, WM. PRICHARD, 1783.

The Reconciliation; or, The Triumph of Nature. A Comic Opera.
12mo, pp 48. *Philadelphia*, PRICHARD & HALL, 1790.

McHENRY, JAMES.

DR. JAMES MCHENRY, born in Larne, County Antrim, Ireland, December 20, 1785; died there July 20, 1845. He was graduated in medicine at Dublin University and Glasgow, and first located in practice at Larne, whence he removed to Belfast. He came to the United States in 1817 and followed his profession in Baltimore, Md., and Pittsburgh, Pa. In 1824 he settled in Philadelphia, where he practiced medicine and carried on a mercantile business. From 1842 to the time of his death he was United States Consul at Londonderry, in Ireland. His home in Philadelphia was the resort of most of the literary people of that and other cities. He published a poem on the "Pleasures of Friendship" in 1822. He was editor of the "American Monthly Magazine" in Philadelphia in 1824, and wrote and published a number of novels.

J. M.

The Usurper. A Historical Tragedy.
> *Philadelphia*, 1829.
> Played at the old Chestnut Street Theatre.

MEAD, ———.

Wall Street; or, Ten Minutes before Three. A Farce.
> 3d Edition. 18mo, pp 34. *New York*, 1819.

MEGIA, F.

La Fayette en Mount Vernon en 17 de Octubre, 1824. Drama in Two Actos.
> 16mo, pp 30. *Filadelfia*, STAVELY Y. BRINGHURST, 1825.

MERRY, ROBERT.

ROBERT MERRY, born in London in April, 1755; died in Baltimore, Md., December, 1798, was educated at Harrow and Christ Church College, Cambridge. Entered at Lincoln's Inn; on the death of his father he gave up the law and bought a commission in the Horse Guards as a lieutenant. He soon quitted the army and went to the Continent. For some years he resided at Florence, where he was a member of the Della Cruscan Academy.[1] Was a good poet and prolific writer. Married Miss Brunton, the celebrated English actress, in 1792. In 1796 they came to Philadelphia, where Mrs. Merry resumed her profession with great applause and took the first place as an actress. Of him Mr. William B. Wood says: "No man possessed less quite." He wrote several plays in England, but his only dramatic work in America was: —

IN MANUSCRIPT.

The Abbey of St. Augustine.
    Played for the first time in Philadelphia in 1797.

MILNE, ———.

IN MANUSCRIPT.

All in a Bustle; or, The New House. A Prelude written for and acted at the opening of the New Theatre (The Park), New York, January 29, 1798 (Dunlap's Management).

1 *Della Crusca*, of the *Seine*, as they went to sift literature.

Flash in the Pan. A Farce.

> Played at the Park Theatre, New York, 1798.

The Eclipse. A Farce from the author's comedy, The Comet.

The Portrait Painter. A Dramatic Monologue, with Sketches of a Beau, a Belle, a Miser, an Epicure, a Real Fine Lady, etc.

> Performed at the Park Theatre, New York, May 25, 1798, by Mrs. Melmoth.

MINSHULL, JOHN.

A Comic Opera, Entitled Rural Felicity, with the Humour of Patrick and the Marriage of Shelty.

> 8vo, pp 68. *New York*, 1801 (Portrait).

A Comedy Entitled; The Sprightly Widow, with the Frolics of Youth.

> 8vo, pp 64. *New York*, 1803. Portrait of Author.

She Stoops to Conquer; or, The Virgin Triumphant. A Comedy in Three Acts.

> 8vo, pp 34. *New York*, 1804.

A Comedy Entitled, The Merry Dames; or, The Humorist's Triumph over the Poet in Petticoats, and the Gallant Exploits of the Knight of the Comb. A Comedy in Three Acts.

> 8vo, pp 30, *New York*, 1805.

MORRIS, GEORGE POPE.

GEORGE POPE MORRIS, born in Philadelphia, Pa., October 10, 1802; died in New York City, July 6,

1864. In association with Samuel Woodworth he founded the New York "Mirror" in 1823. With N. P. Willis he instituted the "Home Journal" in 1846. He was a graceful and popular writer, and is especially remembered for many favorite songs. A complete edition of his poems was published in 1860.

J. M.

IN MANUSCRIPT.

Briar Cliff; A Tale of the Revolution. A Drama.

Played at the Chatham Theatre, New York, June 15, 1825.

MUNFORD, ROBERT.

COLONEL ROBERT MUNFORD was a distinguished patriot of the Revolution. His poems and plays were collected and published by his son William, noticed below.

The Candidate.

The Patriots.

The above plays were published in a volume of Minor Poems, at Petersburg, Va., 1798.

MUNFORD, WILLIAM.

WILLIAM MUNFORD, son of the above, was born in Mecklenburg County, Va., in 1775, and died in Richmond, Va., June 21, 1825. At the age of twenty-one he was elected to the Virginia House of Delegates. He was afterwards a senator from his district, was elected a member of the Privy Council of State, and continued in that office up to the time of his death. His chief literary work was a " Translation of Homer's Iliad," in blank verse, which was not published during his life-time.

Almoran and Hamet. A Tragedy. Published in a volume of Poems and Compositions in prose on Several Occasions.
  Richmond, 1798.

MURDOCK, J.

The Triumphs of Love; or, Happy Reconciliations. A Comedy.
  [Plate.] 12mo, pp 83. *Philadelphia,* 1795.

NEAL, JOHN.

JOHN NEAL, born in Portland, Me., August 25, 1793; died there June 21, 1876. He was entirely self-educated, and, after a few years of business occupation in Baltimore, he was admitted to the Maryland Bar in 1819. He had already begun to have some popularity as a writer of stories, and in 1823 he was led to make a trip to England, in consequence of the popularity which his novels had acquired there. While in England he wrote several articles on America for the " Quarterly Review," and enjoyed an intimacy with British men of letters, particularly Jeremy Bentham. On his return in 1828 he established "The Yankee," and was an active journalist for half a cen-

10

tury. To his energy is attributed the agitation of woman's suffrage, and the establishment of gymnasiums. He was Poe's first encourager. His " Recollections" were published in 1869.— *J. M.*

Otho. A Tragedy in Five Acts.
> 16mo, *Boston*, 1819.
>
> This play was written for Edmund Kean. It was entirely re-written in the " Yankee " for 1828.

NOAH, MORDECAI MANUEL.

Mᴏʀᴅᴇᴄᴀɪ Mᴀɴᴜᴇʟ Nᴏᴀʜ, born in Philadelphia, July 19, 1785; died in New York, May 22, 1851, was a journalist and a lawyer. He went into politics when quite young, and was appointed United States Consul to Morocco in 1813. Came to New York about 1820, and edited "The National Advocate." He afterwards established " The New York Enquirer," " The Evening Star," and other papers. He published also a volume of travels. He was at one time appointed sheriff of the county. An estimate of his character and popularity is thus given by a contemporary : " He told the best story, rounded the best sentence, and wrote the best play of all his contemporaries. . . . As editor, critic, and author, he was looked up to as an oracle."

The Fortress of Sorrento. A Petit Historical Drama.
> 18mo, pp 28. *New York*, 1808.
>
> Taken from the French opera of " Leonora."

She Would be a Soldier; or, The Plains of Chippewa. An Historical Drama in Three Acts.

18mo. *New York,* 1819.

This piece was written for the benefit of Miss Leesugg. It was finished in three days, and first played in Philadelphia in 1813. It was performed at the Park Theatre, New York, June 21, 1819.

The Wandering Boys; or, The Castle of Olival. A Melodrama in Two Acts.

16mo. *Boston,* 1821.

This was also played under the name of " Paul and Alexis; or, The Orphans of the Rhine." It was written for Mrs. Young's benefit, and played at Charleston in 1812.

Marion; or, The Hero of Lake George. A Drama, founded on the events of the Revolutionary War, in Three Acts.

16mo. *New York,* 1822.

Played at the Park Theatre, New York, November 25, 1821.

The Grecian Captive; or, The Fall of Athens. A Drama.

18mo, pp iv.–48. *New York,* 1822.

Played at the Park Theatre, New York, June 17, 1822.

IN MANUSCRIPT.

Siege of Tripoli.

Played at the Park Theatre, New York, May 15, 1820.

The Park Theatre was burned on the night of the author's benefit, May 25, 1820, supposedly in consequence of inflammables used in this play. Mr. Noah gave back his share, over four hundred dollars, to the managers for distribution to the actors.— *J. M.*

NORVAL, JAMES.

The Generous Chief.   A Tragedy.

> 8vo.   *Montreal*, 1792.
>
> This is, probably, the only original play published in Canada prior to 1831.

PARKE, JOHN.

JOHN PARKE was born in Delaware about 1750. At the commencement of the Revolution he entered the American Army and was attached to Washington's Division.   After the war he was for some time in Philadelphia, and was last heard of in Arundel Co., Va.   A number of the pieces in his book are dated at camp in the neighborhood of Boston, at Valley Forge, and other places.

Virginia.   A Pastoral Drama, on the Birth Day of an Illustrious Personage and the Return of Peace, February 11, 1784 (4 lines of poetry in Latin).

> *Philadelphia:* Printed by ELEAZER OSWALD, at the Coffee-House, 1786.
>
> Published in a volume of poems entitled, "The Lyric Works of Horace," etc.
>
> Another edition. *Philadelphia*, ELEAZER BALDWIN, 8vo, pp 14, 1789.
>
> This is probably the first attempt to celebrate Washington's Birthday.

PAULDING, JAMES K.

JAMES KIRKE PAULDING, born in Pleasant Valley, Dutchess Co., N. Y., August 22, 1779; died in Hyde

Park, in the same county, April 6, 1860, was associated with Washington Irving in literary work on "Salmagundi." A paper on political affairs from Paulding's pen led to his appointment by President Madison as Secretary of the Navy Commission in Washington. He was Agent of the Navy at New York, 1825, and Secretary of the Navy under Van Buren.— *J. M.*

The Bucktails; or, Americans in England.
A Comedy, written shortly after the conclusion of the War of 1812.

This play was published in a volume entitled "American Comedies," by W. I. PAULDING, Author; CAREY & HART, Publishers. *Philadelphia*, 1847.

PAYNE, JOHN HOWARD.

JOHN HOWARD PAYNE, born in New York City, June 9, 1791; died in Tunis, Africa, April 9, 1852, was an actor and journalist. In early life he removed to Easthampton, L. I., where the greater part of his childhood was passed. He played in a number of amateur performances, and made his début as an actor at the Park Theatre, New York City, February 24, 1809, as *Young Norval*. He made his literary début by contributing to "The Fly," a juvenile paper published by Woodworth. He soon after published a little paper called "The Thespian Mirror," which had a short existence.

After playing in a number of American cities he went to England in 1813, where his success as an actor and dramatist was very great. His first appearance was at Drury Lane Theatre, June 4, 1813, as *Norval*. He also started a periodical in London called the " Opera Glass."

He returned to America in 1832 and contributed to the " Democratic Review " and other periodicals. Soon afterward (1841) he was appointed United States Consul at Tunis, where he died.

Julia; or, The Wanderer. A Comedy in Five Acts, as performed at the New York Theatre.

    16mo, pp 72. *New York*, 1806.

    The first separate writing of Payne, written over the pseudonym " Eugenius " when he was 14 years of age.

    Performed as " The Wanderer " at the Park Theatre, New York, February 7, 1806.

Lover's Vows. A Play in Five Acts.

    16mo. *Baltimore*, 1809.

Brutus; or, The Fall of Tarquin. An Historical Tragedy in Five Acts.

    8vo, pp viii.–53. *London*, 1818–19.

    16mo. *New York*, 1819.

    Acted for the first time at the Theatre Royal, Drury Lane, London, December 3, 1818.

    First acted in the United States at the Park Theatre, New York, March 15, 1820.

Accusation; or, The Family of D'Anglade. A Melodrama in Three Acts, from the French, with alterations.

    18mo, pp vii.–76. *Boston*, 1818.

    First acted at Park Theatre, New York, May 10, 1816.

Therese, The Orphan of Geneva. A Drama.

18mo. *New York,* 1821.

First acted at the Anthony Street Theatre, New York, April 30, 1821.

Adeline; or, Seduction. A Melodrama in Three Acts.

16mo, pp 41. *New York,* 1822.

Performed for the first time in the United States at the Park Theatre, New York, May 1, 1822.

Clari, the Maid of Milan. An Opera in Three Acts.

16mo, pp 54. *New York,* 1823.

Another Edition. 8vo, pp 45. *London,* 1823.

Performed for the first time at the Theatre Royal, Covent Garden, London, May 8, 1823.

In this opera " Home, Sweet Home," was sung for the first time.

Performed for the first time in the United States at the Park Theatre, New York, November 12, 1823.

Ali Pacha; or, The Signet Ring. A Melodrama in Two Acts.

18mo, pp 36. *New York,* 1823.

Performed at the Park Theatre, New York, May 8, 1823.

Richelieu; or, The Broken Heart. A Domestic Tragedy founded on Fact. (As adapted for performance at the Theatre Royal, Covent Garden, London, before it was altered by order of the Lord Chamberlain, and produced under a new name.) Now First Printed from the Author's Manuscript.

18mo, pp 79. *New York,* 1826.

The Two Galley Slaves. A Melodrama in Two Acts.

18mo, pp 33. *London*, N. D. (1823). Frontispiece.
First performed in the United States at the Park Theatre,
New York, October 27, 1823.

'Twas I; or, The Truth a Lie. A Farce in Two Acts.

8vo, pp 15. *London*, N. D.
Another Edition. 18mo. *New York*, 1828.
First performed in the United States at the Park Theatre,
New York, May 20, 1826.

Charles the Second; or, The Merry Monarch. A Comedy.

18mo, pp 45. (*London*, N. D.)
Another Edition. *Philadelphia*, 1829.
First performed in the United States at the Park Theatre,
New York, October 25, 1824.

Love in Humble Life. A Petit Comedy.

18mo, pp 31. *London*, N. D.

The Lancers. A Farce.

18mo, pp 27. *London*, N. D.
Played at the Park Theatre, New York, 1829.

The Fall of Algiers. A Drama.

18mo, pp 28. *London*, N. D.

Mrs. Smith; or, The Wife and the Widow. A Farce, adapted from the French.

8vo, pp 20. *London*, N. D.
Played at the New Park Theatre, New York, March 6,
1825.

Peter Smink; or, The Armistice. A Comic Drama, adapted from the French.

8vo, pp 16. *London*, N. D.
Played at the Park Theatre, New York, October 14, 1826,
as " Peter Smink; or, Which is the Miller ? " A Farce.

IN MANUSCRIPT.

Oswali of Athens.

Proclamation.

PEPPER, GEORGE.

Kathleen O'Neill, Ireland Redeemed; or, The Devoted Princess.
  Philadelphia, N. D.
  Played at the Lafayette Theatre, New York.
  (The Lafayette Theatre was burned on the night of April 10, 1829, and never rebuilt.—*J. M.*)

PERCIVAL, JAMES GATES.

JAMES GATES PERCIVAL, born in Berlin, Conn., September 15, 1795; died in Hazel Green, Wis., May 2, 1856, was an eminent geologist. He was graduated from Yale College, studied medicine and practiced in Charleston, S. C. Was appointed surgeon in the United States Army in 1824, and stationed in Boston, Mass., on detail for the recruiting station there. He left the service, and took up the study of geology at New Haven, Conn., in 1827. He aided Noah Webster in the compilation of his dictionary. He was an official geologist of Connecticut and of the State of Wisconsin.— *J. M.*

Zamor. A Tragedy.
  12mo, pp 346. *New Haven*, 1820.
  This play formed part of the Commencement exercises at Yale College in 1815. It was afterwards published in Percival's first volume of poems (" Prometheus," etc.).

11

PHILLIPS, J. O.

The Female Spy.
Played in New York in 1828.

Paul Clifford.
Played at the Park Theatre, New York, September 25, 1830.

Beauty and Booty.

PIRSSON, J. P.

The Discarded Daughter,
New York, 18––?

POTTER, REUBEN.

Phelles, King of Tyre; or, The Downfall of Tyranny.
A Tragedy in Five Acts, as performed at the New York Theatre.

16mo, pp 76. *New York,* 1825.

Acted three times at the Park Theatre between June 13 and 28, 1825.

IN MANUSCRIPT.

Don Alonzo.
A Tragedy.

PRESTON, WILLIAM.

Louis XVI.
A Tragedy in Five Acts.

New York: Printed by T. & J. SWORDS, 1794.

RITTENHOUSE, DAVID.

Miss Sara Sampson. A Tragedy, translated from Lessing.

    8vo.   *Philadelphia*, 1798.

ROBINSON, J.

An actor and member of the old American Company.

IN MANUSCRIPT.

The Yorker's Stratagem; or, Banana's Wedding. A Farce in Two Acts.

    Played at the John Street Theatre, New York, in May, 1792.

ROGERS, DANIEL.

The Knight of the Rum Bottle & Co.; or, The Speechmakers. A Musical Farce in Five Acts, by the Editor of " The City Hall Recorder."

    18mo, pp 16.   *New York*, 1818.

    Daniel Rogers was the editor of " The City Hall Recorder " at the time this play was published.

ROGERS, ROBERT.

ROBERT ROGERS was born at Dunbarton, N. H., 1727; died in London about 1798. During the French and Indian War he commanded the celebrated " Rogers Rangers," and participated in the siege of Detroit against Pontiac and the French. Roger's Slide at Lake George is named after him. He went to London about 1764, and was appointed Governor of

Michilimackinac in 1765. He afterwards went to
Algiers and fought under the Dey. He returned to
America in 1775, and professed to be in sympathy
with the patriots, but Washington ordered his arrest.
He then threw off the mask of friendship, and raised
a company of royalists called "The Queen's Rangers."
He went back to England, and his subsequent history
is unknown. His best known works are his "Journal
of the French and Indian War," London, 1765, and
"A Concise Account of North America," London,
1765.

Ponteach; or, The Savages of America. A
   Tragedy.
   8vo, pp 110.   *London:* Printed for the author, 1766.

ROWSON, SUSANNA.

SUSANNA ROWSON, born in Portsmouth, England,
in 1762; died in Boston, Mass., March 2, 1824. She
was an only daughter of Lieutenant William Haswell,
of the British navy, who was, at the beginning of the
Revolution, attached to the Revenue service, and resided at Nantucket, near Boston. His property was
confiscated by the Continental authorities, and himself
and family removed on parole to Hingham in 1775,
and in 1777 to Abington. A cartel was finally ar-
ranged by which Lieutenant Haswell was exchanged,
and sent back to England with his family. Miss
Haswell took employment as a governess in early life,
and was greatly devoted to literature. She married

William Rowson, a musician in one of the bands of the household troops. About the time of her marriage she wrote and published a novel entitled "Victoria," which she dedicated to the Duchess of Devonshire, who introduced her to the Prince of Wales. She was enabled, by this acquaintance, to obtain a pension for her father. On account of the financial embarrassment of her husband, they went on the stage in 1792, in Edinburgh. In 1793 they came to America, and first appeared in Annapolis, Maryland. Thence they went to the theatre in Philadelphia, and, after a season there, became members of the Federal Street Theatre in Boston. Mrs. Rowson, who had, in 1790, published in England the celebrated novel, "Charlotte Temple," had continued writing, and the extraordinary popularity of her story of the unfortunate English girl made it easy for her to follow the cultivation of letters. She retired from the stage in 1797, and established a school for young ladies which remained, during her lifetime, the most select and popular in New England. Her last appearance was in May, 1797, in her own comedy, "Americans in England." Her "Poems" were published in Boston in 1804, and "Lucy Temple," a sequel to "Charlotte Temple," appeared in 1828.— *J. M.*

Slaves in Algiers; or, A Struggle for Freedom. A play interspersed with Songs, as performed at the New Theatres, in Philadelphia and Baltimore.

12mo, pp 74. *Philadelphia,* 1794.

The Female Patriot. A Farce.

    12mo. *Philadelphia* (?), 1794.

    Played in Philadelphia in 1795.

The Volunteers. A Farce, founded on the Whisky Insurrection in Pennsylvania.

    12mo. *Philadelphia*, 1795.

Americans in England. A Comedy.

    12mo. *Boston*, 1796.

    This piece was acted for Mrs. Rowson's benefit and farewell to the stage.

IN MANUSCRIPT.

Columbia's Daughters. A Drama.

    Played at the Mount Vernon Gardens, New York, September 10, 1800.

SAWYER, LEMUEL.

LEMUEL SAWYER was a native of North Carolina. He wrote a "Life of John Randolph" of Roanoke, N. Y., 1844. Died 1844.

Blackbeard. A Comedy in Four Acts, founded on fact.

    16mo, pp 66. *Washington*, 1824.

The Wreck of Honor. A Tragedy.

    16mo, pp 86. *New York*, 18—.

SELDEN, ALMIRA.

Naomi. A Sacred Drama in Five Scenes.

    16mo, pp 152. *Bennington, Vt.*, 1820. Published in a volume of poems entitled "Effusions of the Heart."

SEWALL, JONATHAN MITCHELL.

JONATHAN MITCHELL SEWALL, born in Salem, Mass., in 1748; died in Portsmouth, N. H., March 29, 1808. He was graduated from Harvard and first entered business life, but eventually became a lawyer. He was Register of Probate for Grafton Co., N. H., in 1774; author of the song "War and Washington," very popular during the Revolution. His "Miscellaneous Poems" were published in 1801.

At a performance of Addison's "Cato" in the Bow Street Theatre, N. H., in 1778, an epilogue, written by Colonel Sewall, was spoken, the closing lines of which are,

"No pent up Utica contracts your powers,
  But the whole boundless Continent is yours."— *J. M.*

A Cure for the Spleen; or, Amusement for a Winter's Evening. Being the substance of a conversation on the times over a friendly tankard and pipe, between Sharp, a country Parson; Bumper, a country Justice; Fillpot, an Innkeeper; Graveairs, a Deacon; Trim, a Barber; Brim, Quaker; Puff, a late Representative. Taken in shorthand by Roger de Coverly.

8vo, pp 32. *America,* 1775. (A Tory protest against the Revolution.)

Another edition with the title, Americans Aroused in a Cure for the Spleen, etc. 8vo, pp 32. *New York,* Reprinted by JAMES RIVINGTON. N. D. (1775.)

SIMMONS, JAMES WRIGHT.

JAMES WRIGHT SIMMONS, born at Charleston, S. C. He studied at Harvard and made an extensive tour of

Europe, whence he came to New York and was for a
time a writer for the New York " Mirror."   He was
also connected with other New York papers.   He
afterward held the office of Comptroller General and
Treasurer of the Republic of Texas.   Died at Memphis, Tenn., aged 68 years.

Julian.   A Dramatic Fragment.
  12mo.   N. P. N. D. (1823).

SMITH, CHARLES.

CHARLES SMITH was born about 1768.   He was for
a time a bookseller in New York, and was the editor
of the " Monthly Military Repository."   The following
are all translations from Kotzebue :

The Count of Burgundy.[1]   A Tragedy in Four
    Acts.
  8vo.   *New York,* 1798.
  Another Edition, 8vo, pp vi.–69.   *New York,* 1800.

The Wild Youth.   A Comedy for Digestion in
    Three Acts.
  8vo, pp 74.   *New York,* 1800.

Le Perouse.[1]   A Comedy in Two Acts.
  8vo, pp 40.   *New York,* 1800.

The Virgin of the Sun.[1]   A Play in Five Acts.
  8vo, pp 96.   *New York,* 1800.

[1] All these titles are Dunlap's.   In the list of Dramatic
Authors in the Appendix to Dunlap's History of the American Theatre (First Edition, New York, 1832), Mr. Dunlap
includes this name with the comprehensive line, " Several bad
translations from Kotzebue."— *J. M.*

The Force of Calumny.[1] A Play in Five Acts.
8vo, pp 124. *New York*, 1800.

The Happy Family. A Drama in Five Acts.
12mo, pp 84. *New York*, 1800.

Pizarro; or, The Spaniards in Peru.[1] A Tragedy
in Five Acts.
8vo, pp 62. *New York*, 1800.

The East Indian. A Comedy in Three Acts.
8vo, pp 88. *New York*, 1800.

Indigence, and Nobleness of Mind. A Comedy
in Five Acts.
12mo, pp 64. *New York*, 1800.

The Widow, and The Riding Horse. A
Dramatic Trifle in One Act.
8vo, pp 26. *New York*, 1800.

Abbé de l'Epée;[1] **or, The Orphan.**
8vo, pp 42. *New York*, 1801.

**False Shame; or, The American Orphan in
Germany.**[1]
12mo, pp 63. *Newark* (?) 1800.

SMITH, ELIHU HUBBARD.

ELIHU HUBBARD SMITH, born in Litchfield, Conn.,
September 4, 1771; died in New York, September 21,
1798. A graduate of Yale and physician of Philadelphia, where his father was also a noted doctor.
He wrote a number of Poems and Sonnets for the
magazines. He edited the first collection (1793) ever
made of American poetry. Founder with Drs. Ed-

[1] See note on p. 88.

ward Miller and Samuel L. Mitchell of "The Medical Repository." His death was caused by yellow fever contracted from a patient, a stranger who was taken by him into his own house for treatment.

Edwin and Angelina; or, The Banditti. An Opera in Three Acts.

8vo, pp 22. *New York*, T. and J. SWORDS, 1797.

Played at the John Street Theatre, New York, December 19, 1796. When printed it was preceded by a dedication to Reuben and Abigail Smith, the author's parents.

SMITH, JONATHAN S.

The Siege of Algiers. A Tragi-Comedy.

8vo, pp 140. *Philadelphia*, 1823.

SMITH, RICHARD PENN.

RICHARD PENN SMITH, born in Philadelphia in 1790; died there in 1854. He was educated as a lawyer. For five years he was editor of "The Aurora," and contributed to a number of other periodicals. His books, not dramatic, were a novel, in 1831, called "The Forsaken," in two vols.; "The Actress of Padua and Other Tales." He died August 12, 1854. He wrote fifteen plays in all.

The 8th of January. A Drama in Three Acts.

16mo, pp iv.–54. *Philadelphia*, 1829.

The Deformed; or, Woman's Trial. A Play.

12mo, pp 87. *Philadelphia*, 1830.

The Disowned; or, The Prodigals. A Play.
12mo, pp 67. *Philadelphia*, 1830.

SNAPDRAGON, HECTOR (Pseudonym).

The Russian Banquet. A Drama.
16mo, pp 12. *Boston* (1813).

STEARNS, CHARLES.

CHARLES STEARNS, born in Massachusetts in 1753;
died 1826. He was a Unitarian clergyman, and
from 1785 to his death was pastor of a church at Lincoln, in Massachusetts. He wrote many good poems,
and a variety of religious works.— *J. M.*

Dramatic Dialogues.
12mo, pp 540. *Leominster, Mass.*, 1798.

STOCK, THOMAS.

The Wedding in Wales.
Played in Philadelphia.

STOKES, J.

**The Forest of Rosenwald; or, The Travellers
Benighted.** A Melodrama in Two Acts, as performed at the New York Theatre.
16mo. *New York*, E. MURDEN, 1821.
Another Edition. 16mo. *New York*, 1832.
Played at the Park Theatre, New York, April 26, 1820,
under the title of "The Forest of Rosenwald; or, The Bleed-
ing Nun."

STONE, JOHN AUGUSTUS.

John Augustus Stone, an actor, born in Concord, Mass., in 1801; died near Philadelphia, Pa., June 1, 1834. His first appearance on the stage was made in Boston, and his début in New York occurred July 10, 1822, at the Park Theatre, New York, as *Old Hardy* in "The Belle's Stratagem," and *Old Pickle* in "The Spoiled Child." He was for a long time identified with the Bowery and Chatham Theatres. The prize of five hundred dollars, offered by Mr. Edwin Forrest for the best American play, was awarded to Mr. Stone in 1829, for his drama in verse, "Metamora," long and successfully played by Mr. Forrest. He subsequently received from Mr. Forrest one thousand dollars for his drama, "The Ancient Briton," which, as well as another drama from his pen, "Fauntleroy, the Banker of Rome," were produced by Forrest. He was also author of "La Roque, the Regicide," "Tancred of Sicily," and Yankee Hill's famous play, "The Knight of the Golden Fleece," always the most popular of that comedian's plays. He drowned himself in the Schuylkill River, near Philadelphia, in a fit of mental derangement. Mr. Forrest erected a very handsome monument to his memory.— *J. M.*

IN MANUSCRIPT.

Metamora; or, The Last of the Wampanoags.
A Tragedy.

First produced at the Park Theatre, New York, December 15, 1829.

Philadelphia: From the press of PRICHARD & HALL, in Market Street, between Second and Front Streets. M.DCC.XC. Sm. 8vo, pp xxii.–107 [Plate.]

First played at the John Street Theatre, April 16, 1787.
Reprinted by the Dunlap Society, New York, 1887.

The Georgia Spec; or, Land in the Moon. A Comedy in Three Acts.

8vo. *Boston*, 1797.

This comedy was written to ridicule the speculating mania in wild Yazoo Lands, and was performed in Boston with success.

IN MANUSCRIPT.

May-Day in Town; or, New York in an Uproar. A Farce.

Played at the John Street Theatre, New York, May 19, 1786.

VILLENEUVE, LE BLANC DE.

LE BLANC DE VILLENEUVE was an officer in the French service stationed in New Orleans, La., while that territory was in the occupancy of the French.

J. M.

IN MANUSCRIPT.

Le Père Indien. A Tragedy founded upon an incident in the history of the Calapissa Indians.

Played in 1753 by a company of amateurs in the Governor's Mansion in New Orleans.

WARREN, MERCY.

MERCY WARREN, born in Barnstable, Mass., September 25, 1728; died in Plymouth, Mass., October

19, 1814. She was the third child of Colonel James Otis. She married James Warren, of Plymouth, who was appointed High Sheriff in 1757, which place he held up to the breaking out of the Revolution, when he became general of the American forces about Boston. She was one of the foremost friends of liberty, and corresponded with most of the great men of her time. She published a " History of the American Revolution." Her correspondence with John Adams was published by the Massachusetts Historical Society, 1878.

The Adulateur. A Tragedy, as it is now acted in Upper Servia (6 lines of poetry.)

8vo, pp 30. *Boston.* Printed and sold at the New Printing Office, near Concert Hall, 1773.

The Group. As lately acted and to be re-acted to the wonder of all superior intelligences, nigh headquarters at Amboyne.

Boston. Printed and sold by Edes and Gill, in Queen Street, 1775.

A political satire in two acts in verse, published the day before the Battle of Lexington.

Another edition, 8vo, pp 15. *New York,* JOHN ANDERSON. N. D. (1775.)

The Blockheads; or, The Affrighted Officers.

Boston, 1776.

A counter-farce to Burgoyne's " Blockade." Published without name (attributed to Mrs. Warren) in the " Literary History of the Revolution." *New York,* 1897.

The Sack of Rome. A Tragedy.

The Ladies of Castile. A Tragedy.

> The above plays were published in a volume of "Poems, Dramatic, and Miscellaneous." *Boston*, 1790.

Motley Assembly, The.
> *Boston*, 1779.
> Published without name (attributed to Mrs. Warren), by Paul L. Ford, in "Beginnings of American Dramatic Literature."

WATTERSON, GEORGE.

GEORGE WATTERSON, born in New York in 1783; died in Washington, D. C., 1854. He was a lawyer in Washington, and was the first librarian of Congress. He published several books on law and the topography of Washington. He also published the Letters of General Washington.— *J. M.*

The Child of Feeling. A Comedy.
> 18mo, pp 113. *Georgetown*, 1809.

WETMORE, ALPHONSO.

IN MANUSCRIPT.

The Pedlar. Farce in Three Acts.

WHITE, JOHN BLAKE.

JOHN BLAKE WHITE, born in South Carolina in 1783; died 1859. He was an artist, lawyer and dramatist, residing in Charleston.— *J. M.*

13

Foscari; or, The Venetian Exile. A Tragedy,
as performed at the Charleston Theatre.
    12mo, pp 52.   *Charleston,* 1806.

Mysteries of the Castle. A Drama.
    12mo.   *Charleston,* 1807.

Modern Honour; or, The Victim of Revenge.
A Tragedy.
    12mo.   *Charleston,* 1812.

Triumph of Liberty; or, Louisiana Preserved.
A National Drama.
    12mo.   *Charleston,* 1819.

The Forgers. A Drama,
    Played at Charleston, S. C.   1825.
    Published in "The Southern Literary Messenger," March,
1857, and reprinted New York, 1899.

WHITE, WILLIAM CHARLES.

WILLIAM CHARLES WHITE, born in Worcester,
Mass., made his début on the stage in Boston in 1796,
and in New York at the Park Theatre, January 19,
1801, as Young Norval. He afterwards studied law
and gave up the stage.— *J. M.*

Orlando, or, Parental Persecution. A Tragedy,
as performed at the Theatre, Federal Street, Boston.
    18mo, pp 64.   *Boston,* 1797.   Portrait of Wm. C. White.

The Clergyman's Daughter. A Tragedy in Five
Acts, as performed at the Boston Theatre.
    18mo, pp 96.   *Boston,* 1810.

IN MANUSCRIPT.

The Poor Lodger.
Played in Boston.

WILLIAMSON, A. J.

Preservation; or, The Hovel of the Rocks.
A Play.
   8vo, pp vii.–75. *Charleston*, 1800.

WILMER, LAMBERT A.

Lambert A. Wilmer (born in 1805; died in Brooklyn, December 21, 1863) was editor of the Brooklyn "Saturday Visitor," and of "The Pennsylvanian" in Philadelphia. He was the author of "The Quacks of Helicon."

Merlin. A Drama.
   12mo. *Philadelphia*, 1823.

Gloriana; or, The Enchantress of Elba. A Drama.
   Published in a weekly paper in Philadelphia about 1828.

IN MANUSCRIPT.

The Excursion. A Farce in Two Acts.

Orpheus and Eurydice. A Burletta.

WILLIAMS, JOHN ("Anthony Pasquin.")

John Williams ("Anthony Pasquin") (born in London, England, in 1765; died in Brooklyn, N. Y.,

October 12, 1818). He was educated at the Merchant Tailors' School in London, and was intended for the church. He repudiated that purpose, however, and occupied himself for a time in London with the work of translating for booksellers. He finally went to Dublin, where he engaged in journalism. His methods brought upon him a prosecution, which resulted in his being found guilty, in 1797, as a "common libeller," and subjected to a heavy fine and imprisonment. On his release he came to New York, where he resumed his offensive occupation. He published a volume of poems and several biographies, and a critical paper called "The Dramatic Censor." He was a friend of John Hodgkinson, through whom he obtained an introduction to the stage.

IN MANUSCRIPT.

The Federal Oath; or, Americans Strike Home!
Played at the Park Theatre, New York, June 29, 1799.

Manhattan Stage; or, Cupid in His Vagaries. A Pantomimic Melodrama.
Played at the Park Theatre, New York, April 11, 1806.

WOOD, MRS.

IN MANUSCRIPT.

The North Americans. A Play in Five Acts.

WOODWORTH, SAMUEL.

SAMUEL WOODWORTH (born in Scituate, Mass., January 13, 1785; died in New York City, December 9, 1842). His father was a soldier of the Revolution. In early life he chose the profession of a printer, and went to Boston, where he bound himself apprentice to Benjamin Russell, editor of "The Columbian Sentinel." During this time he employed his leisure in writing poetry for different periodicals in that city over the signature of "Selim." In 1807 he published a weekly paper in New Haven called "The Belles-Lettres Repository." The next year he went to Baltimore, where many of his best poems were published. He came to New York in 1810, and during the War of 1812 published a weekly newspaper entitled "The War." He also edited, at different times, "The Halcyon Luminary and Theological Repository," "The Casket," "The Parthenon," and "The Literary Gazette." He also was one of the founders and editors of "The New York Mirror." In 1816 he published "Champions of Freedom."

The Deed of Gift. A Comic Opera.

18mo, pp 72. *New York*, 1822.

First acted at the City Theatre in Warren Street, New York, January 20, 1823.

Lafayette; or, The Castle of Olmutz. A Drama.

18mo, pp 42. *New York*, 1824.

First acted at the Park Theatre, New York, February 23, 1824.

The Forest Rose; or, American Farmers. A Pastoral Opera in Two Acts.

18mo, pp 42. *New York*, 1825.

First acted at the Chatham Theatre, New York, October 6, 1825.

The Widow's Son. A Play.

18mo. *New York*, 1825.

First acted at the Park Theatre, New York, December 15, 1825.

King's Bridge Cottage. A Revolutionary Tale Founded on an Incident which occurred a few days previous to the Evacuation of New York by the British. A Drama in Two Acts, as performed at the Amateur Theatre.

18mo, pp 23. *New York*, 1826.

WORKMAN, JAS.

Liberty in Louisiana. A Comedy.

12mo. *Charleston*, 1803.

Played at the Charleston Theatre in 1803.

WRIGHT, FRANCES ("FANNY.")

FRANCES WRIGHT (born in Dundee, Scotland, September 6, 1795; died in Cincinnati, O., December 14, 1852). She became, early in life, imbued with French liberalism, and was an admiring friend of Lafayette. She first came to the United States in 1818, and was introduced in literary circles here by Joseph Rodman Drake. After a time spent in Paris

she came again to the United States in 1825, and
purchased 2400 acres of land in Tennessee, at Nes-
hoba (now Memphis).   Here she established a colony
of freed slaves.   The State authorities compelled the
relinquishment of the scheme as contrary to the law
of the commonwealth, and the land which was held
for her in trust by Lafayette was reconveyed to her.
The negroes were sent to Hayti, and Miss Wright
spent three years in lecturing on slavery and social
topics in the United States, especially upon woman
suffrage, of which she was the first considerable advocate.   She went again to France, where she married
Monsieur d'Arnsmont, with whom, however, she lived
but a short time, returning finally to Cincinnati, Ohio,
where she made her final home.— *J. M.*

Altorf.   A Tragedy, first represented in the Theatre
of New York February 19, 1819.
    12mo, pp 83.   *Philadelphia*, 1819.
    This play was produced in different cities, but was not a
success.
    Another Edition.   12mo.   *New York*, 1819.

INDICES

INDEX TO AUTHORS

INDEX TO PLAYS

14*